THE WRITER'S GUIDE TO VIVID SCENES AND CHARACTERS

2022 UPDATED AND EXAPANDED 2ND EDITION

S. A. SOULE

About This Book
UPDATED & EXPANDED 2022 EDITION

Learn Fun and Creative Ways to
Enhance Your Descriptions!

THE ADVICE, tools, and reference lists in this guidebook will inspire writers to create original and vibrant depictions of characters, locations, weather, and mood that can greatly enhance anyone's storytelling, whether you're writing adult, young adult, or children's fiction.

Fictional and real settings are much more effective, dramatic, and evocative when they're visible, auditory, olfactory, and tactile.

Character depictions are much more imaginative, lifelike, and vivid for readers when a character has intriguing physical qualities and distinctive, memorable features.

This valuable reference book offers writers simplified ways to depict vibrant settings and dynamic character descriptions flawlessly. Plus, this edition includes helpful thesauruses on various topics with inspiring word choices!

Please note: Throughout this guide, I use excerpts from my own fiction works to demonstrate how descriptive writing can enhance any scene that I hope you will find inspiring.

Contents

Preface

Fiction Writing Tools appreciates its readers, and every effort has been made to properly edit this guidebook. However, typos, misspellings, and grammar mistakes are occasionally overlooked. If you find an error in the text, please send us an email, so the issue can be corrected. *Thank you!*

http://fictionwritingtools.blogspot.com

Please do not upload this book anywhere for free. That is pirating, and stealing is not cool. Not that you, dear reader, would ever do anything illegal, because you are just too awesome.

Introduction

DEAR WRITER,

I've been writing most of my life, and even though I've studied the craft for years, I still love learning new ways to hone my craft, and I'm assuming that since you purchased this guidebook that you do, too.

In this updated and expanded 2022 edition, I have removed any redundancy and revised some of the outdated information, along with updating the descriptive writing examples and expanding the thesaurus wordlists. I also offer more guidance on creative ways to craft realistic characters and create powerful settings that you can easily and quickly apply to your own writing. And I have included excerpts from my own fiction publications as inspiration, as well as provided modest examples that will give you a better understanding on how to apply descriptive writing to your own stories.

The purpose of this handbook is to ignite your passion for writing and encourage you to craft amazing descriptions of characters and settings.

What qualifies me to discuss this topic? Well, I'm a developmental editor, ghostwriter, and book cover designer with over fifteen years of experience on all sides of the publishing industry. I was a Creative Writing major in college, and I once worked as an acquisitions editor for another publisher, and in the last seven years, I've had the honor of doing developmental edits on numerous manuscripts for indie authors. In addition, I'm a multi-genre fiction author under various pen-names, and many of my books have been featured on Amazon's top 100 lists.

And while this guide is only my own personal opinion on this subject, there are many ways to craft descriptive writing and write in a deeper POV, so please take all of these suggestions to heart, and *only* make the changes that you feel will best suit your writing style and story.

This handbook is definitely not a "grammar do or don't" because honestly, mine is not the best. However, my goal is always for writers to come away with stronger writing and self-editing abilities that will give their audience a more personal reading experience.

Happy writing and revising,

S. A. Soule

After reading this guidebook, please visit my blog for writing, self-editing, and promotional tips, along with a list of author services at Fiction Writing Tools And please browse my premade book covers and custom designs at The Cover Coven

THE WRITER'S GUIDE
TO VIVID SCENES AND
CHARACTERS

Descriptive Writing

"WHEN YOU TELL RATHER than show, you inform your reader of information rather than allowing them to deduce anything. You're supplying information by simply stating it. You might report that a character is "tall," or "angry," or "cold," or "tired." That's telling. *Showing* paints a picture the reader can see in her mind's eye. *Cold?* Don't tell me; show me. Your character pulls her collar up, tightens her scarf, shoves her hands deep into her pockets, and turns her face away from the biting wind...." —*Jerry Jenkins, the author of the bestselling "Left Behind" series.*

IF YOU'VE FINISHED WRITING a novel or short story, then congratulations! That is a huge accomplishment to be incredibly proud of, but now comes the revision work that will *really* make your story shine...

When book reviewers use expressions like "dramatic scenes," or "haunting imaginary," or "vivid prose" to describe the writing, what they're really stating is that the writer has succeeded at descriptive prose and Deep POV.

Description isn't optional in fiction. Every scene should include some details pertaining to the environment. It's imperative to effective world-building. If you can make the settings original and colorful, the description will infuse your fictional world with mood and atmosphere.

For instance, if a new scene starts with two characters talking, and there's no mention of where the scene takes place, then it leaves the reader with a weak visual. You don't need to go into too much detail, but some description is helpful in order to cement the scene and keep the characters from seeming as though they're just floating around in space, instead of being firmly anchored to the fictional world where they exist.

This guide will help you create a distinct and realistic world filled with three-dimensional characters, colorful locations, and naturalistic weather, along with sensory details that will arouse the reader's own senses of sight, touch, hear, smell, taste, and even feel.

Now, let's review what you'll learn in this guidebook, which encompasses many topics, including:

The importance of using sensory details (five senses)

Thesaurus of descriptive words

How to revise description info-dumps of places and characters

How to expertly master descriptive writing

The impact setting can have on a story

How to effectively describe life-like characters

How adding color will strengthen descriptions

How using the weather can create mood and atmosphere

How the five senses can deepen the narrative

How nature can enrich the background

ANY FICTION WRITER who has taken a creative writing course, or received a professional edit on their manuscript, or worked with a critique partner has undoubtedly heard these three words: *show, don't tell.*

Descriptive writing is a way of *digging deeper* into a scene that allows the reader to effortlessly imagine your story-world, as well as the characters. Although Deeper POV is considered active writing, it can also be more wordy; however, please don't let that hinder you from using it.

Telling is when a writer provides the reader with direct facts in a straightforward manner. It is best used to summarizes events that aren't really significant to the plot, but are necessary to fill in plot holes or get the info across quickly to keep the story moving forward. Furthermore, *telling* is an outdated form of writing that often creates info-dumps that will bore the modern-day reader.

There are many ways to *show*, such as through the author's use of language (voice,) through their syntax and word choices, sensory details that appeal to the reader's senses, figurative language that incorporates similes and metaphors to help put a specific image into the reader's mind.

Showing merely means allowing the reader to deeply experience things for themselves, through the viewpoint and perception of a character. Descriptive writing is just depicting everything that your character is feeling, observing, and identifying, along with whatever they're seeing, hearing, touching, and/or smelling.

Now, I'm not suggesting to show or describe *everything* in great detail because that would be overwriting and create pacing issues. The key is to intelligently decide when to *show* and when to just *tell*. Finding a balance is necessary.

PLEASE COMPARE THIS SIMPLE EXAMPLE...

BLAND: The sun was setting and it grew dark.

While it states a fact and describes the setting, it's rather dull and a form of telling. Let's see if I can enhance this description.

REVISED: Long shadows yawned and stretched as the sun sunk below the horizon.

The revision is much improved when compared to the first example and enhances the prose by *showing* rather than *telling*.

The reader should always become deeply connected with the images and experiences being recreated by the writer and described by the characters. There are times when *telling* is simply necessary, so it shouldn't be completely removed from your manuscript because that would be impossible and cause some of the prose to become too wordy or awkward.

Just remember as you revise your own work that there are times when *telling* will add to the rhythm of your sentences and is simply necessary. Keep in mind that *telling* shouldn't be completely removed from your writing because that would be impossible.

In my opinion, fiction is mostly about establishing a visceral, emotional connection between the character(s) and the reader. One way to do this is by *showing* instead of *telling*. You can learn to use descriptive writing to *show*, which creates vibrant and dramatic images within the reader's mind that will deeply immerse them in your fictional world.

Personally, I love writing descriptions of settings and characters, but as a freelance fiction editor, I notice that the majority of writers with whom I've worked with forget to include any details regarding the setting or descriptions of their characters. While I'm reading and evaluating their work, I'm not connecting to the story if I can't envision the setting (where the story unfolds or where a scene happens), or visualize the characters.

In the early drafts of a manuscript, *telling* is expected. It's more important to get the story finished, then to worry about if you are *showing* enough. It's during the revision stage that you should be sure to apply descriptive writing.

One way to help readers experience the story through the senses of our characters is by engaging the five senses. Bland sentences with filter words will have the opposite effect.

Please compare these simple examples...

FILTERED: I touched the dress and felt the fabric.

While it states a fact and describes the sense of touch, it's lackluster, right? Let's see if I can improve this description.

REVISED: My fingers caressed the silky fabric.

Not terribly original, but it's better than the first example. Let's review more ways you can apply descriptive writing.

IF YOU'RE GOING to describe how something tastes, sounds and looks, then you can leave out how it feels and smells. You never want to assault your reader's senses.

Descriptive writing is always much more powerful and explicit than just *telling* the reader, but it can often be more wordy. Yet I wouldn't let that hinder your use of this amazing tool.

The descriptive writing examples provided in this guide are for inspirational purposes only and are a tool to get your own creativity flowing to come up with innovative ways to describe your character's physical appearance and settings.

And, dear reader, grammar is definitely not my forté, so please forgive any overlooked issues in the text. Despite that, I know that the advice I provide will give you clever ideas on ways to revise your settings and create more realistic characters.

Additionally, I'd like to make one more point, there is absolutely nothing wrong with using "appeared" or "seemed" in your sentences on occasion to avoid passive writing, and I use the term "filtered" and "bland" to convey a form of telling or a dull description.

The purpose of the examples and my novel excerpts throughout this guidebook are to encourage you to describe your characters and settings in more creative ways, so I genuinely hope that they inspire your inner-muse.

In the next several chapters, I'll share simple and fun ways that you can incorporate sensory details into your settings and strength your world-building that will give your readers a vibrant image of the locations within your storyworld.

3

The Five Senses

"FILTERING WORDS ARE GENERALLY words that you add to a sentence when you are trying to describe something that your character is experiencing or thinking. These can be sense words like *feel, taste, see, hear,* and *smell,* or variations thereof. Writers don't necessarily have to avoid these words, but they should be aware of the effect that they have on your prose. Rather than describing a sensation outright, you are distancing your reader from the sense that you are describing." — *Corrine Jackson, young adult author*

FICTIONAL AND REAL settings are much more effective and dramatic when they're visible, auditory, olfactory, and tactile. That's why sensory details can enrich any setting through the descriptive use of smells, colors, textures, sounds, and the sense of touch/feel.

World-building is a critical and necessary part of any work of fiction. All descriptions need specific, concrete details, so that the reader can visualize what is being described or experienced by the characters through one or more of the five senses.

To describe life-like characters and settings, you should incorporate the senses in your descriptions. Remember that "telling" a reader what a character is seeing, hearing, touching, or tasting is *not* descriptive writing and takes your prose out of a deeper POV.

Powerful descriptions should always strive to involve the use of every human sense. It's also a great way of making all of your scenes three-dimensional.

The main senses are:

Sight: Show the reader what your character sees by describing the setting through their eyes. For instance, illustrate the glint of sunlight on a stained glass window or the shiny, black wings of a raven.

Hear: Noises that surround your character(s) in every scene, like a dog howling or an old furnace grumbling, or the blaring horn of a car speeding by.

Smell: Describe the scents, aromas, and odors. For instance, reveal the scent of clean laundry, freshly cut grass, or the aroma of orange blossoms.

Touch: Let the reader feel the textures of the character's surroundings. For instance, you can show the icy feel of snow, the touch of rough bark on a tree, or the luxuriousness of silk sheets.

Taste: Depict the tastes of your character's world. For instance, describe the tart flavor of a lime, the sweetness of melting chocolate, or the harsh burn and acrid taste of whiskey.

WHEN DESCRIBING the setting take into consideration the different sensory elements within each scene. Make every effort to illustrate the scenery for readers by using some of the five senses listed above. For instance, describe the coldness of a bathroom floor, along with the interlacing stench of perspiration and the flowery scent of deodorant of a gym locker-room, or the fragrant aroma of a rose garden.

Descriptive writing removes bland storytelling and cranks the narrative up a notch. If done correctly, it rids a story of unneeded phrases, for example *he thought, he knew, he heard, he smelled, he felt* (when it applies to emotions), *he wondered, he saw, etc.* that cause author intrusion. One way to get readers emotionally invested and emerged within your story is to use specific words to describe how things smell, how certain foods taste, how objects feel, how the setting sounds, and also looks through your character's eyes.

HERE ARE a few great ways to make your settings more significant for the reader...

Be specific whenever possible

Being accurate in your descriptions will make it effortless for the reader to imagine your world. Don't just state there was a car, but say he drove a battered, green BMW. It's not a hat, but a blue baseball cap. Don't just state it was a street, but describe it as a gravel road or an abandoned neighborhood. Rather than tell the reader there was a big house, describe it as a colossal mansion that dominated the estate.

Use distinctive nouns and verbs

Do your best to avoid using ambiguous adjectives that label an object or describe a location. A specific verb or noun will anchor any description in a more effective way. Explanatory labels are words like *pretty, mature, amazing, significant,* or *incredible.* Instead find descriptive adjectives; *shabby, frizzy, rough, tattered,* or *overgrown.*

Adjectives can bring help breathe life into the narrative and even stimulate the reader's imagination. Often a combination of sensory details and adjectives can be used to create a very powerful image of a scene in the reader's mind.

Research any real locations

For settings based on actual locations, the Internet is one of the easiest places to do quick and easy research. For instance, a search online for "Houston, Texas" will bring up numerous websites that provide travel information, facts, and the state's history.

Or use Google Maps to get a sense of the location, or do an image search and browse photos. Read a book on the history of a city or town. You can even look up words for example like "California vacation" or "travel journal" to gain a wealth of knowledge about a certain place through reading the personal accounts of a trip.

Of course, if you're writing a historical narrative, extremely detailed research is needed to avoid inaccuracies. A visit to your local library can be helpful to research a particular time period or era throughout history.

Use sensory details

Do your best to include a few sensory details experienced by the point-of-view character, so the reader will be able to clearly envision colors, temperatures, odors, and even the feel of textures. Descriptions that include the senses are an important part of great writing and memorable prose.

Sensory details help the reader feel as though they are experiencing everything alongside the character, and it will create a much more intimate connection to the scene. The senses can also help to set the mood and ping the theme, while establishing a strong "narrative voice."

Lastly, have fun with your descriptions!

In the next several chapters, I will go over innovative ways to integrate the five senses into any fictional setting.

4

Sight

"DESCRIPTION IS OFTEN necessary to let your readers know where the characters are in the story. In TV and movies, a change of scene is often signaled by a brief shot of the place from the outside. Sometimes you can skip this by just having a phrase such as "3 p.m. Wednesday, OK Corral" at the top of a scene, but even then, you may want to add words describing the dust, the tumbleweeds and the acrid smell of gun smoke." —*author, Victoria Grossack, Writing World*

"Sight" is one of the main senses that a character would use to describe a place or another character.

Each time you state that a character enters a new scene describe their surroundings and use the sense of sight to indicate the colors, shapes, and images that they see.

Optical details that appeal to the sense of *sight* can ensure that the reader is able to imagine characters, and add tangible specifics to a setting. For instance, a room can become more than just a vacant, ambiguous receptacle.

Through the characters "eyes," it becomes a room with dark wood paneling, oval windows, and a tarnished hardwood floor.

A graphic description allows readers to place themselves *within* the scene, so including sensory details like "sight" to the narrative will help the reader to easily imagine the character's environment.

However, always strive to omit any filter words: *see / saw / could see* from the narrative. And avoid overusing "looked" or "appeared" in your descriptions. Alternatives could be: *viewed, regarded, observed, spotted, glimpsed,* or *catch sight of,* etc.

PLEASE REVIEW these descriptive writing examples...

The sun rising in the distance cast golden beams over the heads of the houses.

Her lush locks of hair had a silky, black gloss.

The shimmery light of the moon created a soft glow above the trees.

A pile of orange, brown, and red autumn leaves littered the ground.

The vampire's pale skin gleamed in the moonlight and his blood-flecked eyes narrowed on my neck.

THE OBJECTIVE of Deep POV is to secure the reader inside the character's head without using filter words that distance your reader.

Please compare these simple examples...

FILTERED: I <u>could see</u> Malcolm walking toward me.

REVISED: Malcolm strode toward me with a brisk gait.

FILTERED: I <u>looked</u> at the forest.

REVISED: The forest was a vast landscape of greenery.

FILTERED: He <u>saw</u> a raccoon walk across the road.

REVISED: A raccoon ambled across the gravel road.

FILTERED: I <u>see</u> the moon lift overhead.

REVISED: The moon hung in an inky sky.

I HAVE INCLUDED a wordlist to use as a reference to offer creative and original ways to describe your settings.

Thesaurus wordlist for describing characters and settings:

Angular

Rangy

Gaunt

Dull

Cloudy

Gloomy

Hideous

Nauseating

Vile

Splintered

Cracked

Fractured

Ashen

Pale

Insipid

Dusty

Grimy

Grubby

Gargantuan

Immense

Immeasurable

Pocked

Dented

Blemished

Spongy

Malleable

Soggy

Elegant

Stylish

Classy

Pointed

Sharp

Jagged

Spotted

Speckled

Patterned

Feathery

Downy

Fluffy

Jutting

Protruding

Overhanging

Boiling

Fiery

Burning

Prickly

Spiny

Sharp

Steamy

Humid

Sweltering

Knobbed

Knotted

Twisted

Pulpy

Mushy

Soft

Stubbly

Bristly

Bearded

Rocky

Bumpy

Stony

Bubbling

Effervescing

Simmering

Swollen

Bulky

Husky

Flushed

Blushing

Rosy

Lean

Wiry

Sinewy

Ruffled

Tousled

Rumpled

Foggy

Muddled

Hazy

Dense

Impenetrable

Opaque

Furry

Shaggy

Hirsute

Tidy

Clean

Polished

Flawless

Immaculate

Spotless

Fuzzy

Nebulous

Shadowy

Lopsided

Uneven

Irregular

Translucent

Transparent

Cluttered

Chaotic

Strewed

Shimmering

Iridescent

Glistening

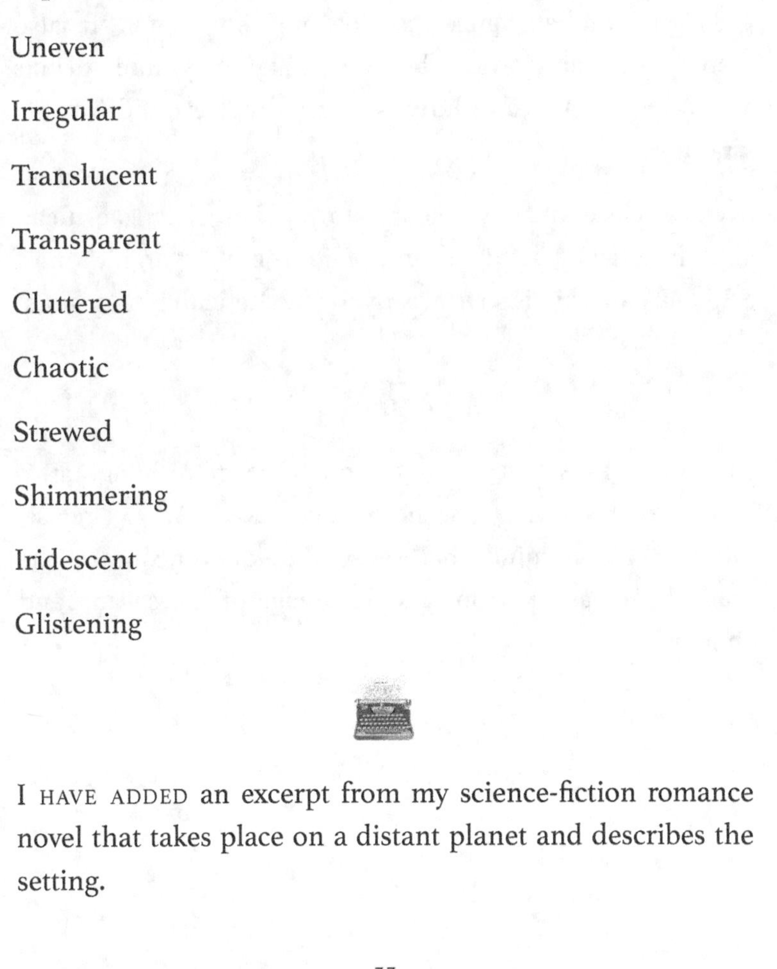

I HAVE ADDED an excerpt from my science-fiction romance novel that takes place on a distant planet and describes the setting.

Please review this descriptive writing example...

Two hours later, I'm chilling with Viola on lounge chairs near a crystal blue pool in the backyard of my dad's strange home on this even stranger planet. The best part of this trip so far is our house, an ultra-weird, metal monstrosity with all sorts of windows that poke out and stare down on us, looming at the end of a private driveway.

The house has a built-in touchscreen panel in each room that controls lights, heat, and other high-tech wonders, and even the kitchen faucet is not only for water. It also dispenses ice and various beverages, like the yummy drinks Viola and I are currently sipping, and even drinkable vitamins.

My eyes close and my face tips toward the clear, caerulean sky. I'm wearing a shirt over a plaid mini-skirt and a ton of SPF. My pale skin is so *not* ready for the Reticuli binary suns.

THIS CHAPTER SHOULD INSPIRE you to be more imaginative whenever describing a scene or a character. As you revise, please keep in mind that sensory details encourage the reader to create a strong mental image of the setting and characters.

5

Sound

"HEARING" is one of the most common senses to use in description. Whenever your character hears a noise or the scene changes to a new location, the sense of hearing should be applied when depicting the scene to provide the reader with more sensory details.

The sense of *hearing* is an important means of communication for your characters. Next to visual details like *sight*, auditory sensations should be included in every genre, no matter where or when your imaginary story takes place. This is because sounds will give the reader an essential experience of the fictional world, while creating a dramatic images in their minds.

Common filter words are *heard / hear / could hear* that can create narrative distance. And if your reader already knows in whose POV the scene is written, then why would you need to explain what he/she is hearing?

The sense of hearing can be a powerful trigger for your characters. While writing a descriptive setting, consider the memories that music can produce, or the sound of a lover's voice, or the jangle of the ice cream truck when you were a child. Certain loud sounds can make a person wince or tense up, while other softer noises can make us relax and smile.

A scene that includes the sense of hearing and sounds is much more likely to induce an emotional reaction in the reader. Including sounds that a character hears will help the reader to strongly envision the surroundings.

Please review these descriptive writing examples...

Flying over the wheat field, the haunting caw of a crow filled the air.

The fussy baby's wailing echoed off the nursery walls.

The shriek of a firetruck's siren resounded in the town.

The bacon frying in a pan sizzled and spat.

Rain trickled down the windowpane likes a child's tears.

Do your best to avoid overusing the words: *sounds* or *sound*. Alternatives could be: *noise, hum, echo, thud, reverberation, crash, jingle, clatter,* or *vibration,* any of which are more specific for the reader.

Please review these descriptive writing examples...

FILTERED: Kate heard the distant sound of a train.

REVISED: The train's piercing whistle sliced the air.

FILTERED: He <u>hears</u> a yowling <u>sound</u> coming from the bedroom.

REVISED: A yowling seeps from beneath the closed bedroom door.

FILTERED: She <u>heard</u> the <u>sound</u> of the car coming.

REVISED: The Ford's tires screeched, kicking up gravel on the road.

NOT ALL FILTER words should be completely removed from your prose because that would be difficult, so if using a filter word like "sound" in the sentence creates easier readability and avoids passive writing, then I would leave it. I also think it's perfectly okay to use when describing a tone of voice in dialogue.

Below, I have added a brief excerpt from my urban fantasy mystery novel that describes the setting through a few of the five senses.

Please review this descriptive writing example...

I hiked through the woods until I reached the cemetery. One lamplight flickered near the opening as I slipped into the darkness of Blackmoor Crypts. The ancient cemetery was in the middle of the forest, surrounded by tangled under-growth and a dense grove of trees. Using the flashlight app on my phone, I swung the light around to orient myself. Faint moans drifted on the wind like insidious whispers.

A crackling twig rang out in the stillness.

I held my breath, listening hard. Most likely an animal. Another branch snapped and I whirled. "Who's there? Dante?"

A shadowy figure moved into the moonlight. I started to scream, but a hand clamped over my mouth.

I HAVE INCLUDED a list of descriptive "sound" words to use as a handy reference whenever describing what the character is hearing.

Thesaurus wordlist to describe sounds:

Banging

Cracking

Hushing

Rapping

Snarling

Barking

Crashing

Jangling

Rasping

Snoring

Bawling

Croaking

Jingling

Rattling

Stuttering

Belching

Crunching

Ringing

Tapping

Blaring

Crying

Moaning

Ripping

Tearing

Booming

Dripping

Rumbling

Tinkling

Burping

Exploding

Mumbling

Rustling

Thudding

Thumping

Buzzing

Fizzing

Scratching

Scraping

Chattering

Gagging

Ticking

Chiming

Gasping

Noisy

Screeching

Twittering

Chirping

Warbling

Clanging

Grating

Piercing

Wheezing

Clapping

Growling

Pinging

Clicking

Grunting

Plopping

Popping

Clinking

Gurgling

Splashing

Cooing

Hissing

Quacking

Squawking

Whizzing

Coughing

Honking

Snapping

Whooping

THE ADDITION of auditory awareness in any scene gives the writer the opportunity to create a more detailed, layered, and textured setting.

6

Smell

THIS CHAPTER DISCUSSES the filter word "smell," and how omitting any filtering references from your prose will improve your writing. Common overused words are *smell / smelled / smelling / could smell* that get abused in my humble opinion.

The sense of smell is generally neglected in fiction writing. However, it's the sense of smell that is most intimately linked to the brain. The receptors in the brain that are responsible for processing odors are also close to the area that's in charge of memory storage. Because of this link, smells are able to trigger intense memories. And the sense of smell has an especially strong influence over our moods, reactions, and emotions.

The awareness of "smells" can be a fun way to add an extra layer of complexity and realism to your descriptions. And smell is a natural reaction that can be included in almost every scene that you write. The human sense of *smell* has the extraordinary ability to evoke a strong response in readers by producing a memory or emotional reaction, and often remind them of their own personal experiences such as the fragrance of a woman's perfume, the scent of freshly brewed coffee, or the stink of rotting garbage.

Smell can help a character to appreciate the aroma of a home-cooked meal, the whiff of freshly washed hair, or the scent of spring flowers. But it can also be a warning system, notifying a character to certain dangers, like smoke, rotten food, or dangerous chemicals.

The sense of smell can affect the setting, and create a strong response for both the reader and the characters. Smell incites sensory details that will help the reader to strongly envision the character's surroundings.

Please review these descriptive writing examples...

The aroma of cut grass lingered in the playground.

The mouthwatering scent of freshly baked cookies came from the kitchen.

In the locker room, the stench of sweat and unwashed hair made Janice's nose wrinkle.

I caught a whiff of pine from the Christmas tree.

Pungent gas fumes crammed the air of the urban city.

HERE ARE MORE examples to illustrate the use of *smell* in your own stories.

Please compare these simple examples...

FILTERED: Lori could smell the tree scents in the air.

While the first example states the facts and describes what the character smells, it's rather dull, isn't it? Let's see if I can revise this bland description.

REVISED: Aromas drifted from the meadow—pine and cedar—as a strong gust blew across the rippling lake.

My revised version is a nice improvement when compared to the first example. Let's look at a few more illustrations.

Please compare these simple examples...

FILTERED: I smelled the chicken burning on the stove.

REVISED: A burning odor wafted from the stove.

FILTERED: I smelled sulfur filling one corner of the room.

REVISED: A sulfurous odor rose from a corner of the room.

BELOW I HAVE INCLUDED a handy wordlist to use as a reference to describe a character's surroundings.

Thesaurus to describe smells:

Anosmatic

Deodorizing

Halitosis

Inodorous

Anomic

Fresh

Heady

Muscatel

Osmic

Gamy

Hircine

Nasal

Deodorized

Indurate

Aroma

Aura

Balm

Fragrance

Incense

Odor

Redolence

Savor

Scent

Smelly

Spicy

Perfume

Bouquet

Pong

Whiff

Waft

Reek

Tang

Pong

Sniff

I HAVE INCLUDED an excerpt from my YA urban fantasy novel that uses the sense of smell in the description.

Please review this descriptive writing example...

We moved past open doors along the corridor, each room decorated in mid-nineteenth-century Victorian chic and into the library. The familiar scent of polished wood and musty books tainted the air. In one corner sat a mahogany desk cluttered with books and ledgers. My purse sagged on its surface where I'd last left it.

THIS IS a short excerpt from my adult urban fantasy includes the sense of smell.

Please review this descriptive writing example...

He froze and we both gazed at my hand on his arm. Slowly, he lifted his head. Our gazes locked and the world around us faded away. I stared into those ice-blue eyes and felt a rush of heat flow between us. His scent wrapped around me in masculine notes of warm amber and cinnamon bark. Lowering my hand, I moved closer, feeling inexplicably drawn to him.

ANOTHER FUN and creative list of "smell" words to use as a reference while describing settings in any fictional world or characters.

Thesaurus for describing diverse smells:

Stinky

Stench

Acidy

Acrid

Antiseptic

Aromatic

Balmy

Biting

Bitter

Briny

Burnt

Citrusy

Comforting

Corky

Damp

Dank

Distinctive

Earthy

Fishy

Flowery

Fragrant

Fresh

Fruity

Gamy

Gaseous

Heavy

Lemony

Medicinal

Metallic

Mildewed

Minty

Moldy

Musky

Musty

Odorless

Peppery

Perfumed

Piney

Pungent

Putrid

Reek

Rose

Rotten

Savory

Scented

Sharp

Sickly

Skunky

Smoky

Sour

Spicy

Spoiled

Stagnant

Stench

Stinking

Sulphur

Sweaty

Sweet

Tart

Tempting

Vinegary

Woody

Yeasty

Clean

Fresh

Fragrant

Fragrance

Crisp

Juicy

Refreshing

Unpolluted

Strong

Perfume

Cologne

Aftershave

Toilet Water

Body Spray

Whiff

Sniff

Bouquet

Tinged

Pungent

Spicy

Overpowering

Smelly

Reeking

Fetid

Malodorous

Rank

Putrid

Noxious

Rancid

Medicinal

Musty

Pungent

Bitter

Burning

Rotten

Salty

Smoky

Sour

Spicy

Stale

Stinky

Odor

Tang

ANYTIME YOU CAN REMOVE A SENSORY "TELL" from a scene and clearly state whatever it is the character smelling, it will enhance the scene.

Just remember as you're revising any scenes in your manuscript that the addition of olfactory details can also help to establish the mood by triggering the senses.

7

Touch

THE HUMAN SENSE of *touch* can provoke a sensory response in the reader. It allows the reader to feel the softness of a warm, freshly washed towel, the abrasiveness of a brick wall, or the prickly stab of a cactus in bloom. It lets the reader sense the sharp, cold slap of winter winds on the hero's skin, the scorching blaze of a roaring fire in a hearth, or the itchy feel of an old wool blanket.

Texture describes the way something feels when touched with a character's hands, fingertips, or skin. I've noticed in the manuscripts that I critique, and often in the books I read, the sense of "touch" is one the most unused descriptors.

To give readers a clear image of the setting, try to include the sense of touch. Dr. David Linden states that the human brain has evolved to have two distinct yet parallel pathways for processing touch information. The first is a sensory pathway, which gives us the facts about touch, vibration, pressure, and fine texture. The second pathway processes social and emotional information, determining the emotional content of mostly interpersonal touch using different sensors in the skin. This pathway activates brain regions associated with social bonding, along with the pleasure and pain centers.

The sense of touch can encourage a character to investigate the world around them by feeling objects and discovering the texture, shape, and size. Tangible images can be powerful sensory triggers if used correctly. They allow a reader not only to visualize a scene, but to experience it.

Please review these descriptive writing examples...

My hand gripped the bottle of sticky syrup.

The Egyptian cotton sheets felt like lying on a soft and luxurious cloud.

Karen gripped the steaming mug of coffee, winching as it burned her fingers.

She sat on the freshly mowed grass, the bristly stalks pricking her skin.

When he grabbed a bag of ice from the freezer, the coldness made him shiver.

WRITING with filter words such as "I touched the cat's fur" or "It feels soft" is almost never necessary in a deeper POV. Instead, simply describe the feeling of the object. Alternative words could be: *stroked, handled, sensed, experienced, caressed,* or *contacted,* etc.

And while using the word "touch" or "touched" in a sentence isn't necessarily wrong, it can create narrative distance on occasion.

Please review these simple examples...

FILTERED: I felt cold when I stepped outside.

While that filtered example states the facts and describes the weather, it's dull. I'll try to revise this bland description.

REVISED: The chilly winds nipped at my cheeks and I shuddered.

The revised sentence is more graphic and visual compared to the first example. Let's consider more ways that you might revise filtered sentences.

Please review these simple examples...

FILTERED: I felt the cat's soft fur coat.

REVISED: I stroked the cat's silky fur.

FILTERED: I touched the shaggy carpet.

REVISED: My fingers caressed the thick shag carpeting.

FILTERED: She felt the rough bark on the pine tree.

REVISED: Her hand patted the rough bark on the towering pine.

FILTERED: The ocean waves felt icy on my bare skin.

REVISED: The icy waves crashed onto the beach and chilled my skin.

I HAVE ADDED a brief excerpt from my adult cozy para-mystery novel, where the main character can detect lying when she feels a coldness on her neck.

Please review this descriptive writing example...

A tingle of coldness slapped my nape. He was lying. He wasn't disappointed at all.

"*Really?*" I said, eyeing him closely. "So, you thought maybe there was a chance there could've been a spark between you two? And when Angela stood you up, maybe you got angry..." I let the implication dangle in the air between us.

"And murdered her?" Nate blinked, as if hearing this accusation had startled him awake. "*No!* I was only distraught to discover the potential love of my life was dead."

My intuition was shrieking like a wailing banshee. The chilly sensation spread to my shoulders, freezing my skin.

"You're lying," I accused.

Nate's eyes widened. "Why would you say that?"

"Because you are. I know it," I blurted without thinking.

I HOPE those examples encouraged you to revise your own descriptions.

This list of textures and descriptors should be used as a vital reference when describing something the character touches or feels, and offer different and creative word choices.

Thesaurus to describe textures:

Abrasive

Ragged

Serrated

Notched

Blunt

Dull

Rounded

Unsharpened

Scarred

Scratched

Scraped

Grooved

Broken

Fragmented

Cracked

Indented

Dented

Bubbly

Foamy

Soapy

Fizzy

Frothy

Soft

Mushy

Slushy

Squishy

Bulging

Bulky

Massive

Hulking

Compact

Bumpy

Lumpy

Ribbed

Ridged

Rutted

Crisp

Crunchy

Brittle

Crumbly

Brisk

Nippy

Bushy

Shaggy

Hairy

Luxuriant

Cold

Cool

Freezing

Frigid

Icy

Chilly

Chapped

Corrugated

Grooved

Uneven

Ridged

Wet

Damp

Clammy

Moist

Saturated

Slimy

Slippery

Spongy

Springy

Mushy

Dry

Dusty

Sooty

Wither

Dehydrate

Encrusted

Covered

Coated

Caked

Enveloped

Engraved

Etched

Imprinted

Inscribed

Carved

Fat

Thick

Solid

Firm

Hard

Crisp

Dense

Plump

Feathery

Fluffy

Fleecy

Cottony

Fuzzy

Furry

Flimsy

Gossamer

Smooth

Sheer

Silky

Filmy

Swollen

Bloated

Puffy

Inflated

Gelatinous

Jellylike

Sticky

Gooey

Tacky

Glassy

Glazed

Glossy

Slick

Granular

Grainy

Coarse

Rough

Gritty

Coarse

Sandy

Scalding

Burning

Humid

Steamy

Sweltering

Leathery

Stringy

Fibrous

Gristly

Malleable

Rubbery

Flexible

Limp

Narrow

Thin

Slim

Threadlike

Frail

Fragile

Greasy

Grimy

Oily

Oleaginous

Fatty

Ornamented

Ornate

Flowery

Baroque

Lavish

Pointy

Jagged

Razor-sharp

Prickly

Bristly

Itchy

Rusty

Corroded

Eroded

Windswept

Craggy

Scored

Scraped

Scratched

Nicked

Spiky

Thorny

Barbed

Prickly

Acerbic

Waxy

Plastic

Wooden

MOST OF US have heard the saying, *"show, don't tell"* many times. In order for a reader to become deeply involved in a story, they must be able to visualize the setting, hear the sounds, imagine touching the objects, and even smell everything within the scene.

8

Taste/Flavor

SENSORY DETAILS like *taste* can be a great tool for description in any genre. Fiction writing that lacks any descriptions is in peril of becoming dull and uninteresting. Description can create a more concrete and sensory experience for our readers.

It's important to remember as you're revising a manuscript that humans first learn about the world around them through the five senses. They are a person's initial source of knowledge about their surroundings. Consequently, descriptive writing that encompasses sensory details like "taste" is more likely to engage the reader.

By including the human sense of taste, it allows a reader to do much more than simply read about whatever the character is tasting, whether it's food, the atmosphere, or air. Without the insertion of sensory details, the story might seem vague and generic.

The four common tastes are:

Sour, Salty, Bitter, and Sweet

Synonyms for Taste:

Flavor (noun), delectability, deliciousness, flavor, goodness, pepperiness, saltiness, savoriness, sourness, spiciness, sweetness.

Meal (noun), banquet, barbecue, board, bread, consumption, cuisine, dinner, eating, fare, food, foodstuff, ingestion, meal, meat, morsel, nutriment, repast, spread, sustenance.

Eat (verb), bite, breakfast, consume, devour, dine, drink, eat, feast, feed, grub, gulp, ingest, lunch, picnic, snack, sip.

BY DIRECTLY ENGAGING any of these taste sensations, you have the creative opportunity to involve a reader's senses. To paint a vivid picture of the setting include the sense of taste. Sensory details this will help the reader to effortlessly imagine the character's surroundings.

Please review these descriptive writing examples...

Taking a gulp, the bitter sting of whiskey burned his throat.

The tanginess of the orange lingered on her tongue.

The potato chips tasted crisp and salty.

The bubbly soda fizzed in her mouth.

I bit into a chocolate chip cookie, savoring the sugary flavor.

BELOW I HAVE PROVIDED examples of bland versus descriptive writing when using this sense.

Please review these simple examples...

BLAND: She liked the taste of grape juice.

REVISED: She enjoyed the tangy flavor of grape juice.

BLAND: I ate an ice cream cone and enjoyed the chocolate taste.

REVISED: I licked the ice cream cone, the chocolate sweetness melting in my mouth.

HERE IS an excerpt from my YA urban fantasy novel that uses "taste/flavor," along with a setting description.

Please review this descriptive writing example...

Jumping off the bed, I ran into the bathroom across the hall. I brushed my hair, gurgled with minty mouthwash, and put on cherry flavored lip-gloss. Then I went downstairs and out the front door.

I hurried down the porch steps, my new bunny slippers crunching on the crisp leaves. The somber sky was covered by the pinpricks of silvery, blinking dots. I checked the darkest areas surrounding the house. One shadow amid the trees detached itself from the rest. Raze, wearing his leather duster, strode over to stand in front of me.

THIS LIST of textures and tastes should be used as a vital reference when describing something the character eats or drinks.

Thesaurus wordlist to describe different tastes:

Acidic

Acrid

Bitter

Bland

Burnt

Buttery

Chalky

Cheesy

Chewy

Chocolaty

Citrusy

Creamy

Crispy

Crunchy

Doughy

Dry

Earthy

Fermented

Fiery

Hot

Fishy

Fizzy

Flakey

Flat

Flavorful

Fresh

Fried

Fruity

Gamey

Garlicky

Gelatinous

Glazed

Grainy

Greasy

Gooey

Gritty

Herbal

Cold

Icy

Juicy

Lemony

Malty

Mashed

Meaty

Mellow

Mild

Minty

Moist

Mushy

Nutty

Oily

Oniony

Overripe

Peppery

Pickled

Powdery

Raw

Refreshing

Ripe

Roasted

Robust

Salty

Sautéed

Savory

Seared

Seasoned

Sharp

Slimy

Smokey

Soggy

Soupy

Sour

Spicy

Spongy

Stale

Sticky

Stringy

Sugary or sweet

Sweet-and-sour

Syrupy

Tangy

Tart

Tasteless

Tender

Toasted

Tough

Unflavored

Unseasoned

Vinegary

Watery

Woody

Yeasty

Zesty

Zingy

Thesaurus wordlist to describe a flavor or taste:

Amazing

Appealing

Appetizing

Delectable

Delicious

Delightful

Divine

Enjoyable

Exquisite

Extraordinary

Fantastic

Finger Licking Good

Heavenly

Lip Smacking

Luscious

Marvelous

Mouthwatering

Palatable

Satisfying

Scrumptious

Superb

Tantalizing

Tasty

Terrific

Wonderful

Yummy

THIS CHAPTER SHOULD GIVE you imaginative ideas on ways to include the taste sense in your own narratives.

In the next several chapters, I'll discuss ways to describe settings in vibrant details that will give readers a clear image of the places located within your fictional world that will help with world-building.

9

World-Building

"Writers use setting to give characters a place to play out their actions and dialogue, so they don't become "talking heads" adrift in the mists of a vague nowhere land. How unsettling for readers to follow a character's thoughts or story dialogue for several pages, all the while uncertain about the location. How odd that a character would talk or think for pages or paragraph after paragraph without interacting with the objects around him, as if there were none..." —*author and fiction editor, Beth Hill of "A Novel Edit"*

Whether your story takes place in a real location, a parallel universe, a fictional town, or a distant planet, it's important to include details about the cities, towns, and areas where your characters roam. This chapter illustrates ways to describe locales within the narrative.

When crafting descriptions, there's often a continuous struggle between technical accuracy and the story's pacing. If the description of the location is too brief and described in nondescript way, a reader doesn't get a clear image of the story-world, but if it's overly detailed, the descriptions can bore the reader and having them skimming the text.

To vividly depict your storyworld, whether real or imagined, use these scene questions as guides.

For instance, what would your character see out their windows at work or home? Skyscrapers? Victorians? Suburbia? Tree-lined streets? Gravel roads? Spaceships? Cornfields? A vast ocean? Railroad tracks? A quiet village? Bus stop?

What objects would the character notice? Fire hydrants? Kids walking dogs? A taco truck? A newspaper stand? Plants and trees? Cracked sidewalks? Homeless people? Graffiti? Department stores? Hard concrete landscapes? A derelict alley? A congested freeway?

What do the buildings look like? Modern? Historical? Urban decay? Gothic revival? Tudors? Stone structures?

And what businesses would the character view? A hospital? Church? Grocery store? Shopping center? Barber shop? Florist? Restaurants? Factory? Motels?

What does the character hear in their hometown? Big trucks rumbling by? Horns honking? Police sirens? Birds singing? Waterfalls gurgling? People talking on cell phones?

What does the location/setting smell like? Rotten garbage? Stinky cigarettes? Burning leaves? Car exhaust? The aroma of restaurants?

EVEN BLOCKBUSTER MOVIES like *Avatar* have a complex location that writer and director, James Cameron, painstakingly spent over ten years on the world-building. The planet of Pandora not only had a distinctive setting, but a functioning ecosystem, a native species, indigenous wildlife, and a complete backstory. Another example of awesome world-building is the Shire, a region filled with Hobbits, within J. R. R. Tolkien's fictional Middle-earth that comes to life in the film adaptions by Peter Jackson.

As the narrative progresses, introduce only the elements relevant to the scene, the theme, the characters, and the plot. Whenever describing the setting include action and "narrative voice" and sensory details.

I have included a few examples of bland descriptions versus more creative ones.

Please review these simple examples...

BLAND: I lived near the docks in San Francisco.

REVISED: I lived along the noisy, fish-smelling San Francisco docks.

BLAND: Tom stayed in a dumpy motel in a small Mexican town.

REVISED: Tom stayed overnight in a dusty Mexican town, and slept in a motel that should've been called "El Not-so Grande."

BLAND: He walked down the narrow street with quiet homes.

REVISED: He ambled along the uneven pavement with dark, uninhabited houses lining the street.

THIS EXCERPT IS from my adult urban fantasy novel, "Shadow Magic," that describes a spooky mansion-like college dorm in a fictional supernatural setting.

Please review this descriptive writing example...

Harbinger Hall was a sprawling four-story Victorian mansion akin to a rabbit warren of long, narrow corridors and rooms stuffed with antique furniture made of heavy wood. I opened the stained-glass door and entered, the heel of my boots clacking against the polished hardwood flooring. The lobby had dark-brown paneled walls, oak tables, floor-to-ceiling bookcases, and plush couches placed near a majestic fireplace. An assortment of taxidermy animals claimed almost every surface, making the room appear creepy yet homey. Students hung out or studied in the vestibule, and the scent of firewood and old books hung in the air.

I hurried to the far end of the lobby, and opened the basement door that led to a narrow staircase, then descended into a vast room with two closed doors. The floorboards were scuffed and unpolished, and one antique armchair huddled in a corner. Against one wall stood a row of washer and dryers where students did their laundry.

Wards protected the first door with a shimmer of magic that resembled barbed wire. The second one was unlocked, and I opened it to find a room filled with unused office furniture.

DESCRIPTIVE WRITING just means painting a detailed picture for your readers through your POV character. How they view the world and describe it is what gives the character their own unique "voice."

Here are some examples that show how *telling* the reader information with filter words will create narrative distance. Instead, strive to make your fictional world as three-dimensional as possible.

Please compare these simple examples...

FILTERED: The forest trees <u>looked</u> tall and huge.

REVISED: Within the vast forest, the towering trees swayed in the breeze and cast lengthy shadows onto the ground.

BLAND: <u>There were</u> lots of tall buildings in this part of the city.

REVISED: The soaring buildings with their concrete heads in the clouds cast long shadows on the sidewalks below.

FILTERED: <u>There was</u> a bad storm coming.

REVISED: The horizon lit up with white light followed by the ominous grumble of thunder.

HERE IS an excerpt from my new adult college romance novel that describes the setting by adding sensory details, colors, character description, and narrative "voice."

Please review this descriptive writing example...

My new roommate and I were polar opposites. Her name was Vanessa and she apparently guzzled energy drinks by the gallon, and her tousled copper hair looked like the "before" picture in a Pantene commercial. At least she seemed nice and normal. I wouldn't have to worry about her doing anything weird like stealing my underwear or taking cell phone pictures of me while I slept to post on Instagram.

Our shared room was enormous compared to my old dormitory. Stevenson Hall had an ancient brick façade, but they'd remodeled the interior to create larger rooms. Apparently, not all dorm rooms resembled dank prison cells with painted cinder block walls. These rooms were more like an expensive apartment than regular campus housing. Even better, the dorms had single-gender floors.

While Vanessa talked a mile a minute, folded clothes on her bed, and sipped a Red Bull, I inspected her—*incredibly* cluttered—side of the room. I flicked a glance at the red poster with that lame phrase "Keep Calm and Carry On" in white lettering over her headboard. Vanessa had fastened a corkboard to the wall above her desk, pinned with snapshots of her high school debate team and blue ribbon awards for science and math. Piles of Old Navy hoodies and graphic shirts and bell-bottom cords were scattered on her dark green comforter.

INSTEAD OF JUST DESCRIBING SOMETHING IN bland detail, try to lace in some of the five senses, emotional responses, "voice," and action to make the description of a setting more powerful and visual for your readers.

Here is an excerpt from one of my adult cozy mystery novel, "Hexes & Hijinks," that describes a storeroom and has narrative "voice."

Please review this descriptive writing example...

Moving further into the room, I stood beside a gurgling water cooler near a bench backed up against the wall. Footfalls creaked from overhead. I swiveled toward the wrought-iron spiral staircase that led to a two-bedroom apartment above Karma Moon, taking up the whole second floor.

PLEASE REMEMBER as you revise your own work that these are only guidelines meant to help develop your own style of crafting dynamic settings and locations.

I hope this advice on world-building helps you to revise your own prose.

10

Evocative Settings

"WHEN WE WRITE about a character's experience in the world, it's natural to want to tell the reader what's being done and how. Maybe the character is noticing something suspicious, maybe they're wondering what the heck is going on, or maybe they're hearing a sound that's out of place. The writer has to convey these insights, but the way it's done can make all the difference. One technique to make these experiences more immediate for the reader is to remove filter words...."—*Crystal Shelley is the owner of Rabbit with a Red Pen, where she provides editing and authenticity reading services to fiction authors*

WORLD-BUILDING ISN'T EASY, but once you learn to create evocative depictions of characters, locations, weather, and mood, it can greatly improve your writing.

Most of my developmental editing clients tend to forget to include any background scenery or description. Or the descriptions are written blandly and have lots of filtering references. As you revise your own work, remember that characters need to be anchored to their settings, and readers need descriptive images to envision the world in which you've created.

A powerful description engages the senses and paints a more compelling image that effortlessly transports a reader into the fictional world that the author has created. Writing that lacks description is in danger of being ambiguous, or even extremely generic, with characters floating around in a black void.

Please review these simple examples...

BLAND: The night was dark.

While the first example states the fact that is a dark night, it's super dull, right? I'll try to revise this bland description into something more interesting.

REVISED: The darkness fell quickly like a shadowy blanket over the land.

My revised sentence is stronger compared to the first example. Let's consider more ways you might craft dramatic scenes.

Whenever depicting a location or setting describe things the way only your unique character sees them through their unique "voice" and sensory details.

Here are simple techniques to make a setting more visual:

Make the landscape active by having characters interact within it.
Use color to add an extra layer of depth to the scenery.
Make the setting a vital part of the scene.
Use the five senses to make the setting more realistic.

I HAVE INCLUDED A LONGER excerpt from my alien romance novel, "Beyond Falling Stars," that takes place on an extraterrestrial planet and uses most of the five senses in the setting description that I hope you'll find inspiring.

Please review this descriptive writing example...

Hayden and I follow the aliens to the hull door, and the creaking sound echoes throughout the spacecraft as the hatch opens and the ramp lowers. We walk outside, and I take my first step into this strange new world.

Warm gusts lift my hair and fill my nose with the fragrant scent of orange blossoms and blooming lilacs, with a subtle bitter green edge. The aromas represent the flora, the flowers, and the seaside landscape. The air feels moist and salty. I step onto the spongy green terrain and my vision drifts upward, squinting into the glare. The gradient cobalt sky has a string of lazy drifting clouds, with dual suns, one much larger than the other, beaming upon the ground and heating my skin.

"Welcome to Reticuli." Zach sweeps out his hand like a game-show host.

We stand near the platform and gape at the scenery. To my left are white beaches, a verdant jungle of foliage, resembling a triple-canopy rain forest with fluorescent leaves, and a calm blue sea, lapping at the shore. If there were any palm trees, I'd swear I landed on a weirdly colorful paradise like the Caribbean or Hawaii.

One deep breath of this phlegmatic atmosphere and my whole body exhales.

In the distance are soaring buildings with paneled walls of mirrored glass, reflecting the twin suns. Their stone heads reach the clouds, casting long shadows on the walkways below.

"What's that city called?" I ask.

"Zoltar," Hayden says. "The biggest metropolitan on Reticuli."

On one side of the urban area, I spot squat domed buildings, which must be homes, all surrounded by strange lavender trees, yellow swaying grass, and weird flowers in vivid pinks, reds, and oranges. There are no cars, but sidewalks, with a slow conveyor mechanism that's transporting the population to different places, which resembles those moving walkways at airports.

A high-pitched screech pierces the air. Grabbing Hayden's arm, I spin on my heel to gaze into the rain forest and notice a rainbow-colored bird cawing from the trees. The cliffside landing strip where the two spaceships parked overlooks the ocean, with its crystal-clear water. Magenta fish swim beneath the surface, and the gold trees with spindly branches in luminous aquamarines wave in the balmy gust.

IF YOU WANT to craft a more compelling read, try to avoid the overuse of sentences starters such as, "There was" or "There are" to describe an object or a setting. These overused words add nothing to the scene, and can make your sentences wordy and dull.

Please compare this simple example...

FILTERED: There was a big table in the dining room and the wood looked like it was rotting. When I touched the surface, it felt rough and dusty.

Sure, a writer can simply *tell* the reader that the room is big and dusty, and it's definitely a faster way to convey details about the setting; however, it makes the prose nondescript and inelegant. I'll do my best to revise that bland description into one that's more powerful and visual.

REVISED: A wooden table huddled in the unused dining room, its surface peeling away like brown bark. As my fingers trailed along its uneven surface, specks of dust coated my fingertips.

Obviously, my simple revision is more vivid than the first example. Let's review another one.

Please compare this simple example...

BLAND: There was a horse and a stack of hay next to its stall.

While it states a fact, it's too bland. Let's see if I can enhance this description.

REVISED: Within the cozy barn, a black mare chewed quietly on a stack of fragrant hay.

Not horrible, and much improved when compared to the first example. Let's review a few more illustrations.

Please compare these simple examples...

BLAND: There are three pictures on the wall in a row.

REVISED: Three framed photos hung in a row on the wall.

BLAND: There were five dogs sleeping on the rug.

REVISED: Five pugs snoozed on the shaggy rug.

BLAND: There were many big, fancy homes in this neighborhood.

REVISED: Impressive mansions with fluted Corinthian columns reigned over the neighborhood.

WHEN DESCRIBING A PLACE OR ROOM, please don't catalog items or furniture like a list of inventory. To successfully create a realistic scene, you need to have your characters interact with the setting, along with including sensory details.

Please compare these examples...

FILTERED: Sarah entered the room. There was a lamp, a couch, a big clock, and letters on the table. She also noticed an awful smell. When she heard the grandfather clock rang out the hour, she was startled.

While the first example states the facts and describes the room to a certain extent, it's bland and has too many filter words, which creates narrative distance. I'll try to improve this rather weak description.

REVISED: Sarah strode toward the dusty antique lamp and switched it on. Muted light illuminated the grimy space, and the unpleasant whiff of mold assaulted her senses. She shook her head at the neglect as she weaved around the velvet sofa and past an oak table that held a stack of unopened mail. When the clock bonged midnight, she flinched.

My revised version of the same scene is more dramatic and creative when compared to the first example. Let's look at another example of unfiltered writing.

I have included an excerpt from a short story that illustrates how descriptive writing can create an evocative setting, include the senses, and cleverly inserts a little backstory.

Please review this descriptive writing example...

Ellen made her way up the rickety steps, the fifth one creaking loudly. As she stepped through the basement door into the airy kitchen, she barely spared a glance at the pile of dirty dishes in the sink or the breakfast bowl sitting on the wooden table surrounded by mismatched chairs that she'd bought at a flea market. The kitchen's yellow painted walls had a dull sheen and the white cabinets, a drab off-white border. A large window faced the field where she could see the wheat swaying like gentle arms waving hello at her. A brief smile touched her lips.

She crossed the tiled floor into the brown-carpeted living room and stood there a moment in the cool, dark space.

The sun slanting through the partially closed curtains cast a long slab of light on the threadbare sofa, where four cats slept. Her grandmother's afghan lay neatly folded across the back and she ran her fingers over the soft fabric. The tall lamp near the side table was turned off and the TV squatting in the corner was silent.

A big tabby sashayed past her, rubbing against her legs on its way to the kitchen and the food bowls. More felines slept in various spots about the room and one had curled up on the rocking chair.

After Ellen's marriage had ended and her grandmother had passed away, she and her thirteen cats had moved into her grandmother's home. The old farmhouse squatted on the edge of town and suited her needs perfectly. Everything in it might be secondhand, but it was *hers*. She'd left every single piece of furniture from her old life behind. This was her fresh start.

A brutal knock on the front door awoke the sleeping cats...

READERS MAY SKIM long pages of unbroken description; however, if it is slipped in as part of the action, then the reader absorbs it almost without being noticed.

11

Vivid Descriptions

"LET your description unfold as a character moves throughout the scene. Consider which details your character would notice immediately, and which might register more slowly. Let your character encounter those details interactively." —*Moira Allen, editor of Writing World and columnist*

IN THIS CHAPTER, I'll discuss ways to make your writing relatable and more vibrant for your readership.

At the beginning of each new scene, I suggest doing a check to make sure that you've clearly established the setting within the first three paragraphs. This is important so that a reader knows immediately the *when* and *where* of the scene. If the characters haven't left a location between chapters, then only briefly mention the setting as a reminder to reorient the reader to the locale.

To reiterate, I strongly recommend describing the setting at the beginning of each new scene and whenever your character(s) goes to a new location.

Revision tips to keep in mind whenever you're revising the setting are:

Do your word choices paint graphic images in the reader's mind?

Do your descriptions place the reader in the scene?

Does your setting make the character an active participant in the story instead of a mere observer?

Did you remember to use a few of the five senses?

WHEN WRITING or revising any descriptions, you can occasionally toss in a few name brands for objects, clothing, and cars, also, you can use specific architectural terms when describing a building or home, and even include the breed of any animals.

After I reading this advice from an online creative writing site, I went through one of my own manuscripts and named most of the streets, used more creative words to describe colors, laced in some brand names, added fabrics to my clothing, named the different animal breeds, and even used a few model types for the vehicles. It really gave my main character more "voice" and my settings a more realistic and detailed feel, and my readers loved the updated edition.

While brand names can be useful in description and make your characters more relatable, if they are overused, then they will distract the reader and might annoy them. Therefore, don't go overboard using brands to label every piece of clothing or product. The occasional use is fine, but most readers don't really care if a character wears Converse with a Nike baseball cap while drinking a Pepsi and watching Netflix on his Kindle.

To recap, as you revise don't forget to name businesses, streets, and cars when necessary. Use architectural styles to describe homes and buildings, and on occasion, toss in a brand name for clothing, products, or objects. And as needed, name the breed of any animals in your story and describe their features.

Please review these examples...

BLAND: I got into my car.

REVISED: I hoped into my convertible BMW.

BLAND: She slipped on a blouse and designer sweater

REVISED: She slipped on a white shirt, and over that she yanked on a red Abercrombie sweater.

BLAND: The older, upscale house had lots of windows and balconies.

REVISED: The lemon painted Georgian-style home had four bay windows facing the front lawn. The second-floor was decorated with cupolas and balconies, giving the exterior an elegant façade.

BLAND: I drove down the street and turned left at the light.

REVISED: I shifted the Camry into drive and sped down Main Street. At the intersection I turned left onto Maple Drive before parking in the empty lot across from Starbucks.

BLAND: My big dog woofed at the mailman, who hurriedly dropped off the mail.

REVISED: Spike, my beautiful German Shepherd, barked at the poor mailman as he shoved the mail into the box.

HERE IS an excerpt from my cozy mystery novel that specifically describes her dog in the opening scene by naming the breed, describing his fur coloring, and even eye color.

Please review this descriptive writing example...

It was after midnight when a thunderous rap shook the door like an anxious fist.

Startled, the paperback I'd been reading tumbled from my hands and clattered to the floor. My fawn-colored French bulldog scrambled to her feet and started barking.

"Shush, Tricksy." I rubbed her furry back. "It's just someone at the door."

Hmmm. Just someone knocking on my door in the middle of the night.

Tricksy quieted down, yet her brown stare stayed focused on the doorway.

THIS NEXT EXCERPT is from my paranormal romance novel, "Immortal Eclipse," that describes a character using a couple of brand names to convey that she's both wealthy and stylish, without blatantly stating it.

Please review this descriptive writing example...

Behind her glass-top desk, Pauletta sits in a sleek black leather chair, which reclines to an almost obscene angle as she crosses her smooth brown legs. She's wearing a silk Hermès scarf draped over a gray blouse, a matching rayon skirt, and a *really* cute pair of Bettye Muller heels.

FOR GENRES LIKE HISTORICAL FICTION, cozy mysteries, fantasy, and science fiction, readers have a tendency to want an intense experience within the fictional world you've created. While world-building, I suggest focusing on reader anticipation whenever describing the setting since it usually plays a big role in the story. However, you don't want to drown the plot in narrative details, so weaving the setting through action, introspection, and dialogue will placate reader expectancy.

Each new scene location should paint a dramatic picture for your readers through your POV character. How they "see" the world and describe it for the readers is what gives them their own unique "voice." Try to include the emotional reactions, internal-dialogue, and physical actions of your characters to spice up your descriptions and avoid a boring list of details. I want to inspire you to *dig deeper* to make your story-world as three-dimensional as possible.

If you use descriptive writing in your own stories, I promise that you'll notice an amazing difference in your prose, and I bet your readers will, too!

Now I challenge you to rewrite a scene and find clever ways to describe your settings, characters, and animals.

In the following chapters, I have more helpful wordlists and thesaurus entries to help you create fascinating worlds that readers will be captivated by.

12

Realistic Locations

"LET your description unfold as a character moves throughout the scene. Consider which details your character would notice immediately, and which might register more slowly. Let your character encounter those details interactively." — *columnist, Moira Allen, editor of Writing World*

THIS CHAPTER EXPLAINS why descriptive writing is one of the best revision techniques that you can use to create a realistic setting through sensory details without giving readers a weak or nondescript visual. The tools and tips in this section will demonstrate easy and fun ways to transform the setting into a much stronger visual.

Locations should be a big part of any narrative, and not merely just a place where the story unfolds. As you revise, remember that all characters need to be associated with their settings. Whatever place you create for your character, he/she must live within it. It's not enough to describe the location or scenery at the beginning of the story, and then let the characters wander throughout the scenes without any further connection to the environment.

By accurately describing the iridescent glint of a raven's wing or the flaming burst of color from a sunrise, you will emerge the reader deeply into the story.

All characters need a place to live and breathe and work and roam. The fictional world (or an actual real place) that you create for your characters should not just include a home, workplace, or neighborhood, but a background as well.

Give readers vital information regarding the setting that include a few additional details, such as the time-period and where the story or scene takes place. *A city in the 1950s? A farm in the 1800s? A high-rise in the 1980s? On a distant planet? In a hellish underground dimension? In the Victorian era?*

HERE ARE some simple techniques to make a setting more visual:

Make the landscape active by having characters interact within it.

Use color to add an extra depth to the scenery.

Make the setting a vital part of the scene.

Use a few of the five senses to make the backdrop more realistic.

Include a mention of the weather and temperature.

Describe the flora and fauna within your storyworld.

WHAT USUALLY DRAWS a reader deeply into a story is the use of language and the way the POV character describes a setting through their unique perspective. One way to do that is to include the five senses in every scene.

Please review these simple examples...

BLAND: There was a big table in the dining room and it looked like the wood was rotting. When I touched the surface it felt rough and dusty.

Too much filtering. In the following revised example, it states the same details, but gives the reader enough of a visual to imagine the table in their mind's eye and experience the "touch" without describing it in a boring way.

REVISED: A wooden table, its surface peeling away like brown bark, sat in the unused dining room. As my fingers trailed along its uneven surface, specks of dust coated my fingertips.

I HAVE ADDED a helpful wordlist to use as a reference when describing your settings and locales.

Wordlist to describe any type of settings:

Desolate

Derelict

Devoid

Enchanting

Ethereal

Colorful

Opulent

Blissful

Blooming

Blossoming

Bright

Sunny

Budding

Cloudless

Flourishing

Floral

Fertile

Fragrant

Grassy

Growing

Lush

Outdoor

Picture-perfect

Rainy

Seasonal

Scampering

Sprouting

Springtime

Verdant

Windy

Breezy

Woodland

Wooded

Earthy

Mountainous

Enticing

Misty

Foggy

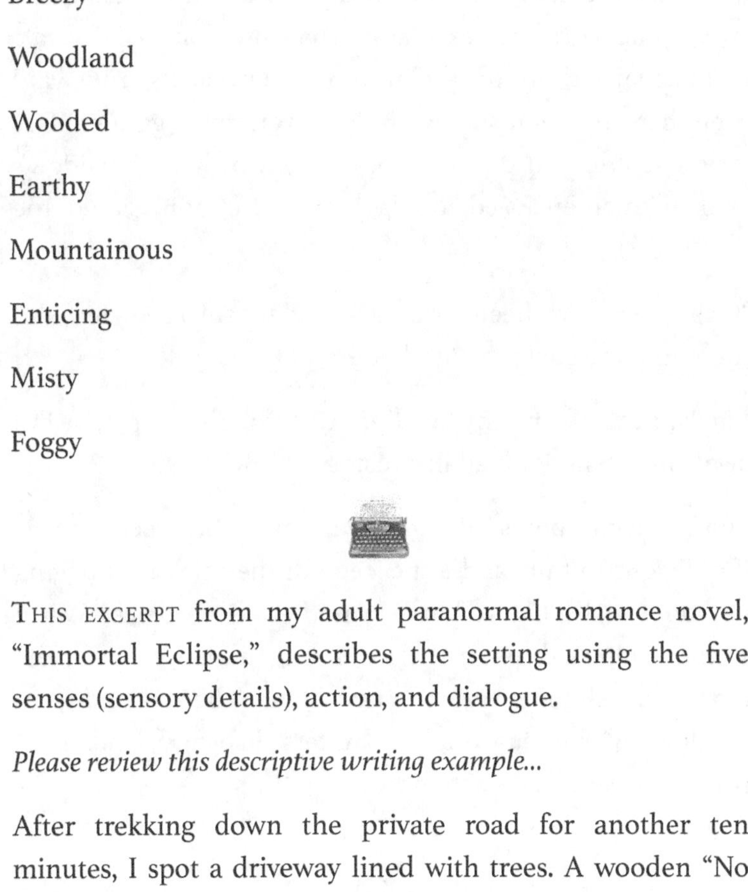

THIS EXCERPT from my adult paranormal romance novel, "Immortal Eclipse," describes the setting using the five senses (sensory details), action, and dialogue.

Please review this descriptive writing example...

After trekking down the private road for another ten minutes, I spot a driveway lined with trees. A wooden "No trespassing" sign is secured to the gated entrance. When I put a hand on the cold iron, it swings open and I slip through the opening.

I hobble along, relieved when a remarkable castle-like building appears, the wood and stone facade speckled with hazy afternoon sunshine.

The mansion stands outlined against the sky, like a hand uplifted in warning, its huge frame dwarfing the pines that form a grove near the property. Weeds and dandelions poke through the cracks in the cobblestone walkway. The impressive mansion resembles a stone bastion from a fairy tale sitting majestically on a cliff above the sea. Its front yard even has the requisite wild and overgrown garden. Dry leaves scuttle and dance across the lawn. A rusty widow's walk, with an enclosed cupola, juts out from one side of the roof.

"Okay, so you've been in a car accident, blacked out, and then time-traveled into another era," I tell myself.

Riiight. I must've hit my head pretty hard. Either that, or I've awakened to find myself in a historical BBC movie.

Summerwind looms over the estate in hushed seclusion, as if oblivious to time and at peace with the thick ivy hugging its stone walls like a lover's smothering embrace. Warm sunlight filters through the trees, but the closer I get, the more goosebumps prickle my skin. The stained-glass windows with their wooden shutters, like heavy lids over stony eyes, seem to watch me.

As a bonus, I have added a useful list of businesses that might be located within your narrative. And don't forget to name each business in your story that the characters visit or frequent.

Places that might populate your storyworld:

Bookshop

Coffee House

Tea Shop

New Age Shop

College / University

Dry Cleaners

Convenience Store

Supermarket

Post Office

Park

Local Shops

Houses

Apartments

Police Station

Bus Stop

Train Station

Subway Station

Cafe

Restaurant

Clinic

Veterinary hospital

Hospital

Community Centre

Retirement Home

Church

Bakery

Gym / Health Club

Tennis Courts

Racetrack

Dentist Office

Pharmacy / Drugstore

Hair Salon

Real estate Agency

Laundromat

Auto Repair Shop

Pet Store

Florist

Toy Store

Bar / Pub

Spa

Shopping Mall

Recreation Center

Museum

Hotel / Motel

Movie Theater

Fire Station

School

Playground

Resort

Gas Station

Prison / Jail

City Hall

Court House

Historical Landmarks

Bank

Grocery Store / Supermarket

Airport

Wildlife Refuge

Gardens

Botanical Gardens

Town Square

Art Gallery

Zoo

Night Club

Planetarium

Aquarium

Amusement Park

Pizzeria

Cocktail Lounge

Ball Room

Fast food Restaurant

Farmer's Market

Library

MY LAST BIT of advice is to never push "pause" on your story to dump out description details or facts regarding the setting or location. Although, I realize some genres like high-fantasy and science fiction require lots of world-building, the descriptions can still be cleverly inserted in snippets throughout the narrative.

13

Room Descriptions

"...[IF the writer] gives us such details about the streets, stores, weather, politics, and details about the looks, gestures, and experiences of his characters, we cannot help believing that the story is true." —*author of "The Art of Fiction," John Gardner*

ONE WAY to successfully create a great story is to remember to describe the setting at the beginning of each new scene or chapter to help the reader get a visual of the location.

If you effectively describe a rooms or interiors, then you will set the scene and give your readers a clear image of where your characters live and breathe. Try not to catalog items or furniture in a room like a boring grocery list. Do your best to balance the action of the character while describing the interior of a house or the rooms of a character's home.

For instance, what would he/she see in their bedroom or living room? Tables? Leather sofa? Bunkbed? A desk? A pile of old records? A cushioned recliner?

What objects are inside their home? TV? Dishwasher? Family photos? A stack of books? A computer? Knick-knacks?

What is the character's furnishings like? Modern? Antiques? Comfortable and worn? Wood, pine, oak?

What does the character hear in their home? The percolating of coffee brewing? Music playing? The drip of a leaky faucet? Static from a TV? Video games being played?

What does he/she smell inside their home? Dirty laundry? Fresh baked bread? Minty toothpaste? Burnt toast? Buttery popcorn? Moldy attic? Smelly sweat socks? A citrus air freshener? Leather furniture?

Those prompts should help you revise any scene in your current work.

Please review this simple examples...

BLAND: There was an old-fashioned filing cabinet, desk, chair, and lamp.

REVISED: The office décor was outdated, with a rusty filing cabinet leaning to one side, a desk held up by brick legs, a wobbly chair, and a brass lamp covered by a moth eaten shade.

FILTERED: The warm kitchen was large and smelled of baking chicken.

REVISED: The oven warmed the spacious kitchen, and the spicy aroma of chicken filled the space.

FILTERED: The room looked just like she remembered. Holly was instantly transported back to her adolescence because her old bedroom still contained everything from her childhood and even smelled the same.

REVISED: She pushed open the solid oak door and stepped into her childhood bedroom. The same light-blue striped wallpaper with posters of rock bands covered the walls. A queen-sized bed, draped with a sheer curtain dominated the room and the faint scent of lilacs drifted in the air.

HERE'S an example of a room description from my Upper-YA alien romance novel, "Lost in Starlight," that weaves in emotion, character background, and the five senses into the narrative.

Please review this descriptive writing example...

Slinging the strap of my backpack over one shoulder, I climb the stairs to the second-floor, then up another narrow staircase to the third-floor attic. Only one big room up here and it's all mine.

My bedroom has a sloped ceiling with wooden beams arching overhead. Three gothic prints by the talented illustrator Victoria Frances parade over the walls and a poster of my favorite band—*Thirty Seconds to Mars*—hangs over the bed. Sunlight streams through the velvet drapes covering the windows, except for the circular one facing the front of the house. A tangy cheese odor emanates from an open bag of Cheetos left on the desk and mingles with the sweet, almost musky, scent of strawberry incense.

Jinx, my black cat, is sprawled across the scarlet duvet covering the bed. He lifts his head and meows a greeting. I shuffle past the sticker-encrusted desk that rests under one of the windows and holds my MacBook computer and a small TV with a built-in DVD player—perfect for watching late-night horror flicks.

HERE IS a handy wordlist to reference whenever you're describing a room, an interior, or furnishings.

Wordlist for room descriptions:

Empty

Vacant

Barren

Bare

Clean

Polished

Shiny

Refined

Gleaming

Cluttered

Littered

Disorderly

Untidy

Cozy / Cosy

Comfortable

Snug

Affluent

Crowded

Ample

Tiny

Narrow

Dingy

Lonely

Stuffy

Charming

Vast

Old-fashioned

Antiquated

Outdated

Conservative

Conventional

Dreary

Shabby

Modern

Elegant

Victorian

Stylish

Baroque

Fancy

Cheerful

Formal

Elaborate

Opulent

Chic

Ornate

Exotic

Pleasant

Sumptuous

Luxurious

Nautical

Funky

Classical

Rustic

Contemporary

Minimalist

Vivid

Striking

Bold

Asian

Colorful

Eclectic

Tropical

Dim

Muted

Diffused light

Murky

Gloomy

Shadowy

Dusky

Dimly-lit

Tidy

Unkempt

Dirty

Grungy

Imperial

Regal

Moldy

Mildewy

Carpeted

Hard wood

Cavernous

Damp

Haunted

Drafty

Draughty

Furnished

Lofty

Distinguished

Stately

Shuttered

Spacious

Airy

Expansive

Roomy

Sprawling

Stark

Unfurnished

Vaulted Ceilings

Cramped

Imposing

Magnificent

Baronial

Grand

Dusty

Grimy

Filthy

Sooty

Do your best to find creative ways to describe the interiors within your story and avoid using filtering words that remove the reader from the experience. My challenge to you is to rewrite a scene in your story with descriptive writing, and use two or more of the five senses.

14

Neighborhood Descriptions

"...SETTING is more than a mere backdrop for action; it's an interactive aspect of your fictional world that saturates the story with mood, meaning, and thematic connotations." —*veteran writing instructor, Jessica Morrell*

THIS CHAPTER FOCUSES on effectively describing a suburban area or residential neighborhood. While drafting your own settings, try to include some of the five senses, which will allow a reader to enter the scene by inducing an emotional response. Adding descriptive details really doesn't take a lot of extra work, and it's worth it to give your reader a "real" world that they can see, feel, hear, and even touch.

One great way of making a scene multi-dimensional is to *dig deeper.* Have fun with your setting descriptions and make them as real as possible for your readers.

For instance, what would he/she see on their street? Buses? Cars? Teens on bicycles? Flowerbeds? Tall trees? A stream? A subway? Trolley cars? Horses and wagons?

Is the street like? Noisy? Hectic? A bustling farmer's market? A neglected estate?

What buildings or places are near their home? Apartments? Other houses? Retail stores? A school? A fire department? A playground? Botanical gardens? Soccer field?

What are the character's neighbors like? Friendly? Aloof? Nosy? Loud?

What does the character hear in their neighborhood? Dogs barking? Music from a radio? Cars pulling into a driveway? Kids playing? Garage doors opening or closing? Insects buzzing? Rusty chains on a tree swing? Wind chimes?

What does he/she smell in their hood? Freshly mowed grass? Stinky sewer drains? The sweet scent of honeysuckle? Burning rubber from tires? Wet dog? Smoke from a chimney? Meat cooking on a BBQ? Chlorine from a swimming pool?

Those prompts should help you revise any neighborhood settings in your own stories.

Please review these simple examples...

BLAND: The neighborhood and homes looked older.

REVISED: The sunlight cast a shadow on the gaunt spectral homes in this ancient neighborhood.

BLAND: The streets were busy with traffic.

REVISED: The traffic lurched along the smog burdened streets.

BLAND: The houses were quaint and homey looking.

REVISED: The yellow bungalows facing the tree-lined side-walk had lush green lawns and softly jingling wind chimes.

THIS NEXT EXAMPLE is a simple description of a derelict neighborhood that should inspire your own creative muse.

Please review this descriptive writing example...

Charlie shivered as he rubbed his arms against the icy winds sweeping the neighborhood. The sun dipped downward in the distance as darkness edged over the dimly lit streets.

Taking stock of his surroundings, Charlie increased his pace. This shortcut had lead him into a dilapidated part of the city. Storefronts, with the occasional apartment above, yielded to rundown, graffiti-covered buildings with busted-out windows and metal doors. He wrinkled his nose at the stench rising from the sewers. He hurried past an abandoned car, the driver's door left ajar, and wished he'd taken a different route home.

I HAVE INCLUDED a handy wordlist to reference whenever you're describing a residential setting or street or neighborhood within your storyworld.

WORDLIST FOR NEIGHBORHOOD and residence descriptions:

Sidewalks

Residential

Green

Beautiful

Rural

Gothic

Marshy

Respectable

Densely Populated

Dangerous

Crowded

Tree-Lined Streets

Clean

Gloomy

Hilly

Leafy

Urban

Rustic

Upscale

Derelict

Exclusive

Older

Newer

Modern

Classy

Cosy / Cozy

Tranquil

Private

Storybook

Hut/ Shack

Condo

Slum

Mansion / Manor

Castle

Lodge

Villa

Estate

Ranch

Manse

Palace

Château

Country House

Tudor

Medieval

Character

Beachfront

Steeply Pitched Roof

Brownstone

Curb Appeal

Cul-De-Sac

Cottage

Weather-Beaten

Farmhouse

Secluded

Porch

Garage

Gazebo

Pool

Sober / Somber

Vast

Landscaped

Granite

Two-Story

Bay Windows

Arched Windows

Stained-Glass Windows

Grand

Dirty

Business District

Ugly

Noisy

Quiet

Suburban

Suburb

Ghetto

Working-Class

Middle-Class

Lower-Class

Dingy

Rough

Thriving

Rehabbed

Picket Fences

Stone Walls

Hedges / Bushes

Wire Fence

Wooden Fences

Weathered

Iron Railings

Lawns

Pastures

Pond / Stream/ Creek

Beach

Stucco

Grassy Knolls

Squat

Looming

Ancient

Multi-Pane Windows

Wood Siding

Half-Timbered Frame

Divided-Light Windows

Patterned Shingles

Asymmetrical Facade

Flagstone Path

Cement Pavers / Paving Stones

Loose Gravel / Gravel Driveway

Gothic Revival

Italianate

Renaissance

Intricate Trimwork

Curved Woodwork

Leaded Glass Windows

Crow's Nests

Widow Peaks

Ornate

Mansard Victorian

Geometric

Whimsical

Charming

Carved Columns

Spindles

Gingerbread Trim

Wood Planks

Solar Panels

Distinctly Modern

Whitewashed

Sleek

Terraces

Boxy Lines

Dramatic Window Walls

Timbered

Sturdy

Ancestral

Row Houses

Deserted / Abandoned

Isolated

Desolate

Forsaken

Imperial

Thatched

Picturesque

Modest

Gabled

Colonial

Ducal

Obscure

Mysterious

Dilapidated

Bricks

Bright

Friendly

Dense

Earthy

Patio / Deck

Turret / Steeple

Dormer Windows

Sandstone

Cobblestone

Craftsman

Mediterranean

Ranch-Style

French Country

Victorian

Queen Anne

Cape Cod

Sparse

Polluted

Paved

Dusty Roads

I HOPE this chapter helps you revise any bland scenes into tangible descriptions that the reader can experience and visualize.

15

Building Descriptions

"...IT may sound obvious, but plenty of writers launch out into a scene without giving us any descriptive material to place and anchor the action. That early paragraph needs to have enough detail that if you are creating a coffee shop, for example, it doesn't just feel like A Generic Coffee Shop. It should feel like its own thing. One you could actually walk into. Something with its own mood and color. One vivid descriptive detail will do more work for you than three worthy but colorless sentences..." *—Harry Bingham, best-selling crime novelist*

THIS CHAPTER HIGHLIGHTS ways to describe buildings and homes. A more specific depiction with powerful, sensory details is the best way to describe a structure or residence. I want to encourage writers to get inventive when describing the buildings within your storyworld, whether fictional or real.

For instance, what type of buildings would your character notice? Bungalows? Metal crates? Warehouses? Buildings shackled with ivy? Stone constructions?

What objects or views would the character notice? Broken windows? Flaking paint? Wraparound porches? Brick facades? Glass walls? Parking lots? Neon signs? Billboards? Chain-link fences?

What style of architecture are the buildings? Space pods? Classic contemporary? Log cabins? Track housing? Concrete structures?

What does the character hear around them? Birds chirping from a rooftop? The swoosh of a revolving door? The rush of traffic? Lawnmowers cutting grass? A gurgling fountain?

What does he/she smell? Rust? Fresh paint? Musty odors? Glass cleaner?

Those prompts should be useful when describing any structures within your own stories.

Please review these simple examples...

BLAND: The barn looked old.

REVISED: The red barn wilted in the field strangled with overgrown weeds, its paint peeling and its doors hanging off the rusty hinges.

BLAND: The buildings looked tall and made of glass.

REVISED: The skyscrapers stood like modern stalagmites.

I HAVE INCLUDED a short description of a mansion as an illustration.

Please review this descriptive writing example...

The desolated Victorian sat regally beyond the wrought-iron fence like a house from an antebellum storybook. The peeling paint had been damaged by harsh winters and the broken windows were dusty and festooned with decaying cobwebs. Rambling roof shingles fell from their high perch and a grove of dead trees surrounded the decaying estate.

THIS NEXT EXCERPT is a scene from my novella, "Craven Manor."

Please review this descriptive writing example...

Chase walked warily up to the log cabin and paused beneath a dirty window. Lifting his head and peeking inside, he glimpsed a room filled with dusty old furniture. Oak floors and banisters gleamed dully in the sunshine. Going around to the porch, he jiggled the brass doorknob. The door slowly creaked opened and the stench of mold and neglect hit his nostrils. He sneezed and the sound echoed throughout the lonely rooms.

PLEASE CAREFULLY STUDY this excerpt from my adult cozy mystery novel, "Hexes & Hijinks," that describes a small town at night.

Please review this descriptive writing example...

The overcast sky darkened, the scent of pine wafting on the autumn breeze. A light rain sprinkled my red Mini-Cooper snugged up to the curb, which could use a wash. I'd just driven two hours in traffic from Modesto and bug guts and bird poop had splattered the windshield.

I jiggled the shop's doorknob, but it remained shut tight. My knuckles rapped on the door, then I peered through the stained-glass window into the dark building. A neon sign—a psychic hand with stars around it—affixed to the window pitched a pink glow into the main store area.

Huh. I tugged my cell phone from my purse and dialed Grandma Elsie's house number. The call went straight to an answering machine and I hung up, dropping the cell into my bag.

Main Street appeared deserted. The other businesses, antique shops, galleries, and cafes, closed and silent. Historical towns like Mystique, California shut down by nine o'clock. A touristy, mountain town so small there wasn't even a mall or movie theater. Surrounding the area were gold mines, wineries, and the Sierra Foothills, a national forest that seemed to guard Mystique like a treasured secret.

I went around the corner and down a dimly lit alley. The brick building beside Karma Moon had grimy barred windows. A security light over the partially open backdoor illuminated the entrance and shone on a planter-box with thriving greenery.

The shadows shifted and the rusty dumpster leaking unidentifiable fluid at the end of the alley banged into the wall. Startled, I yelped as a figure emerged from the shadows.

I HAVE a list of useful words to describe architecture to use as a reference.

Wordlist of architecture and building terms:

Art Nouveau

Concrete

Ecologically friendly/ Green

Gothic

Innovative

Kitsch

Low-Rise

High-Rise

Multi-story

Post-modern

Iconic

Slum

Dwelling

nouveau rich

Posh

ostentatious Luxurious

Abandoned

Spacious

Majestic

Regal

Stately

Sumptuous

Plush (Informal)

Illustrious

Grandiose

Opulent

De Luxe

Splendiferous (Facetious)

Colossal

Gigantic

Condemned

Immense

Lofty

Towering

Vast

Aged

Antique

Dilapidated

Decrepit

Elderly

Historical

Run-Down

Timeworn

Weathered

Modern

Domestic

American

Classical

Roman

Greek Revival

Ancient

Functional

English

Traditional

Contemporary

Monumental

Ecclesiastical

Colonial

Medieval

Romanesque

European

Byzantine

Baroque

Spanish

Japanese

Parallel

Chinese

Classic

Grecian

Tier

Victorian

Georgian

Progressive

Modular

Urban

Mediaeval

Complex

Rural

Generic

Wooden

Genetic

Modernist

Structure

STRONG DESCRIPTIONS ALLOW a reader to actively participate in the scene and ignite their imagination. And a reader who feels like they're experiencing the narrative, is a reader who won't be able to put your story down.

16

Color Descriptors

"Writing, no matter what kind, must appeal to the reader's imagination. Nothing does that better than painting pictures for the mind. To paint a picture, you must use color! Color is communication at its vibrant best. It evokes memory and creates a connection to the mental image. At a subconscious level, color creates an immediate physiological effect. It can calm, soothe, reassure and lower the pulse rate. Or it can stimulate, excite and send blood racing through the veins. It makes your writing alive and immediate, physically and mentally..." *–author, Gail Hamilton "Color words for Writers"*

A fun and imaginative way to transform descriptions is to add a dash of color. This chapter should inspire you to find creative ways to add vibrancy to your descriptions. With a dash of creativity, it's possible to improve anyone's writing by replacing boring word choices with more artistic ones.

As I edit a manuscript, I find most often that the laziest words are produced when describing any scenes or characters that include colors. Effectively written description can present a clear visual for your reader. By creating a strong image in the reader's mind, they will actually imagine exactly what you're describing. And using color to paint that picture is what a real artist does!

Color is everywhere, and it's the easiest way to add some creative sizzle to an otherwise bland description. I suggest buying a box of crayons and use the names as inspiration. Or go online to visit a paint store and browse all the creative hues and differing shades. Choose the right word, and your reader will have an instant association. Do your best to describe skin tones, hair, eye color, clothing, and settings.

Make every effort to avoid using weak descriptions. For instance, *The dog was black,* or *Her hair was blond*. Instead, use descriptive writing to improve descriptions, such as stating: *The Rottweiler's fur resembled the shade of midnight*, or *Her hair gleamed like golden sunshine.*

Here's an excerpt from my adult cozy mystery novel, "Booked For Murder," that describes a residence with colors and sensory details.

Please review this descriptive writing example...

The multi-colored, one-story Craftsman cottage had loads of charm, with yellow siding and white and green trim. Grass grew on either side of a narrow cobblestone walkway that led to the light-blue painted porch. A small, detached garage sat at the end of the driveway.

Blue Jays chirped from the tree in the side-yard, and the flowering shrubs and plants added a vibrant splash of color. I spied geraniums, lavender, Lethe's Bramble, and lilies. I didn't brew many potions, but the florae might come in handy.

Unlocking the gate, its rusty hinges groaned as we entered the yard. Tricksy paused to sniff an eroded watering can on the lawn.

We proceeded up the steps and onto the portico, ignoring the squeak of protest from the old boards. The door and shutters were a rust-colored red, in addition to the porch swing. Grinning, I could already picture myself relaxing in the evenings and sipping tea while Tricksy chewed on a tennis ball.

I used the key Mr. Bathory had given me to unlock the door and stepped inside my new home, the mild aroma of lemon polish tickling my nostrils.

I HAVE INCLUDED a helpful color wordlist to use as a reference to find creative and original ways to describe settings. These colors can also be used to describe eyes, hair, clothing, objects, and even the climate.

Thesaurus of colors and shades:

Cream: yellowish white, light tint of yellow or buff

Lemon: clear, light yellow

Golden: also gold

Wheaten: fawn or pale yellow

Apricot: pinkish yellow or yellowish pink

Mustard: yellowish brown

Biscuit: pale brown

Fawn: light yellowish brown

Fallow: pale yellow, light brown

Beige: light brown, light gray with brownish tint

Tan: light brown

Buff: yellowish brown of medium to dark tan

Tawny: dark yellowish or dull yellowish brown

Bronze: a metallic brownish color

Sandy: yellowish red

Copper: metallic reddish-brown

Sorrel: light reddish brown

Bay: reddish brown

Rust Red: reddish yellow; reddish brown

Ruby Red: deep red; carmine

Mahogany: reddish brown

Liver: dark reddish brown

Chocolate: dark brown

Dark Brown

Coffee brown

Dun: dull, grayish brown

Light Gray

Mouse: dark brownish gray

Gray: color of ash

Grizzle: gray, devoid of hue

Iron gray: silver-white metallic gray

Slate gray: a dull dark bluish gray

Blue: dark gray

Sable: dark brown, almost black

Black: ebony

IF YOU WRITE in genres such as fantasy, science fiction, horror, or paranormal romance, then often times a character will have an exotic color to their skin, hair, or eyes.

Thesaurus of unique and exotic colors:

Framboise

Tanager

Tuberose

Yarrow

Jacaranda

Lobelia

Mesclun

Amaryllis

Cyclamen

Azalea

Jonquil

Lacewing

Frangipane

Alyssum

Verbena

Citrine

Saguaro

Reynard

Nankeen

Arugula

Armagnac

Persimmon

Shagreen

Alabaster

Amethyst

Carnelian

Cinnamon

Coral

Crimson

Ebony

Emerald

Fawn

Indigo

Lavender

Lilac

Scarlet

Sienna

Silver

Auburn

Azure

Cobalt

Granite

Gray

Slate

Teal

Topaz

Bookmark this chapter as a handy reference whenever adding a splash of color to your settings and character descriptions.

17

Nature Descriptions

"...SETTING is more than a mere backdrop for action; it's an interactive aspect of your fictional world that saturates the story with mood, meaning, and thematic connotations. Broadly defined, setting is the location of the plot, including the region, geography, climate, neighborhood, buildings, and interiors. Setting, along with pacing, also suggests passage of time. Place is layered into every scene and flashback, built of elements such as weather, lighting, the season, and even the hour." —*excerpt from "Between the Lines" by author Jessica Morrell*

SETTINGS ARE the locale and background where the characters act out the events of the storyline. Scenes with bland or diluted descriptions are like actors performing on barren stage against a white backdrop. The story might have interesting character and a thrilling plot, but the reader has no sense of location. One way to describe the setting is to include nature in any outdoor scenes. I don't mean just describing the weather, but also, wildlife, plants, temperatures, bodies of water, insects, and landscapes, or anything else that pertains to the story's environment.

It's crucial to great descriptions to use all the senses, because nature is more than a pretty snapshot. To use a few of the five senses in your scenes, consider how the earth smells after a heavy rain. Or how the forest shades the ground and feels cool, then imagine a beautiful setting, like a field of wildflowers on a warm, sunny day. You could describe how the chill breeze feels on the character's skin. Or the hot touch of a rock that's been left in the scorching sun, or the cold sensation a character feels after touching the water of a rushing mountain river.

While *telling* is less wordy and states the facts, it's almost always better to *show* when it comes to nature descriptions. Powerful settings of nature will create stunning and realistic environments that will emerge readers deeply into your fictional world.

Author Thomas Hardy used nature as a key element in most of his scenes, especially in *Tess of the d'Urbervilles*. Occasionally, the author described the seasons as a mirror of his character's emotional growth as well.

If you're writing about nature in a real location, then I strongly recommend extensively researching the locale to ensure the descriptions are realistic and factual.

In this chapter, I have included a wordlist (in no particular order) to help with describing nature in an outdoor setting.

THESAURUS OF DESCRIPTIVE NATURE WORDS:

Animals

Creatures

Fauna

Birds

Abundant

Aquatic

Arctic

Autumn

Equinox

Spring

Plants

Barren

Beauty

Bees

Boulders

Stones

Bountiful

Brook

Stream

River

Creek

Butterfly

Cave

Cavern

Grotto

Cliff

Precipice

Overhang

Bluff

Climate

Weather

Clouds

Mist

Haze

Coastal

Seaside

Shoreline

Coastline

Combustible

Flammable

Explosive

Crater

Desert

Wasteland

Wilderness

Snow-Capped

Snowfall

Blizzard

Marsh

Swampland

Marshland

Everglade

Wetland

Bayou

Woods

Forest

Woodlands

Thicket

Earthquake

Earthy

Eclipse

Erosion

Corrosion

Escarpment

Evergreen

Flora

Fauna

Fall

Fallow

Farming

Rural

Rustic

Pastoral

Countryside

Urban

Metropolitan

Borough

Fertile

Lush

Fruitful

Bountiful

Fibrous

Flood

Foliage

Greenery

Vegetation

Undergrowth

Shrubbery

Bushes

Glacier

Grassland

Growth

Grassy

Verdant

Habitat

Hail

Horizon

Hurricane

Vista

Volcano

Iceberg

Land

Property

Estate

Territory

Leaves

Logging

Lake

Lagoon

Pond

Sea

Jagged

Magical

Magnificent

Marine

Nautical

Sierra

Meteor

Migratory

Moon

Mountains

Foothills

Highlands

Alps

Blossoming

Bourgeoning

Native

Natural

Neglected

Developing

Growing

Parasitic

Peaceful

Pinnacles

Planet

Globe

Prairie

Savannah

Tranquil

Serene

Radioactive

Reserve

Ridge

Crest

River

Rock

Rotting

Contaminated

Scenic

Picturesque

Season

Solar

Swamp

Summer

Solstice

Terrain

Toxic

Tropical

Trees

Weather

Wildlife

Winter

Twilight

ALONG WITH PROVIDING details to enrich the setting, nature is one of the easiest ways to describe any outdoor scenes.

Vibrant descriptions of nature are a crucial element in any outside setting.

18

Wildlife Descriptions

"BESIDES PETS, animals can serve other purposes in novels, such as birds act off-page as a catalyst to the plot, like in *Pandemic* by Yvonne Ventresca, involving a deadly bird flu. Animals can also serve as a symbolic purpose, such as Simon the pig in *No Surrender Soldier,* and the animals featured in the novel, *Lord Of The Flies* by William Golding."
—*author and blogger, Christine Kohler*

ONE IMPORTANT FEATURE TO include in any outdoor or external setting is the local wildlife. Different types of areas support various kinds of fauna. Squirrels, pigeons, rats, mice, and even domesticated household pets, as well as birds and ducks can all be found in an urban environment. While this chapter mainly focuses on land animals often found in outside settings of cities and towns, it could apply to some villages, remote islands, or rural areas, like farms, too.

Within most cities and towns, there are many natural areas —parks, lakes, wildlife reserves, and bodies of water—that attract various animals. For instance, birds flock into city centers to snack on food crumbs, and aquatic birds like swans, geese, and ducks are attracted to any areas of water, even swimming pools and canals. Rodents often thrive in urban locations due to food waste.

Be sure to research your locations to get a better understanding of which creatures might inhabit the places within your own story. If your story takes place in other countries, such as Australia or Africa, then the animals would obviously be extremely diverse. If your story takes place in a specific location, then please take the time to study the country, region, or state.

I have included a basic list of common animals that might be found in outdoor areas to help describe any settings that include wildlife. However, it only lists some of the fauna that is often found in the United States (North America), but is not exhaustive. Please use the list as a reference to inspire creative ways to describe wildlife within your fictional world.

Thesaurus of descriptive wildlife:

Muskrats

Antelope

Beavers

Moose

Geese

Bald Eagles

Armadillo

Lynx

Shrews/Moles

Elk

Mules

Wild Boar

Woodpeckers

Vultures

Scorpions

Badgers

Rattlesnakes

Ocelots

Sheep

Wild Turkey

Toads/Frogs

Groundhogs

Weasels

Porcupines

Rodents

Raccoons

Cats

Dogs

Mice

Rats

Birds

Bats

Reptiles

Hawks

Rabbits

Chipmunks

Deer

Mountain Lions / Cougars

Bears

Bobcats

Foxes

Snakes

Wolves

Squirrels

Opossums

Pigs

Cows

Horses

Bulls

Chickens

Skunks

Coyotes

Owls

Falcons

Lizards

Alligators

Turtles

Goats

Guinea Pig

Ferret

Hamster

Fauna

Creatures

Beasts

Faunae

Mammals

Swine

WHILE THE SENSE OF "SIGHT" will be the main way to describe the wildlife, I think "sound" should be woven into your descriptions, too. Animals can be vocal or make certain sounds that the character might notice.

Wordlist of wildlife noises:

Barking

Buzzing (bees/insects)

Howling (wolves/dogs)

Baying

Snorting, Oinking, Grunting (pigs)

Screeching

Meowing

Purring

Growling

Squawking, Crying (gulls/birds)

Clucking

Snarling

Rattling (snakes)

Cawing

Mooing

Chirping

Squawking

Quacking

Croaking

Honking (geese)

Bleating (lambs / goats)

Trilling (raccoons)

Neighing, Whinny, Nicker (horse)

Squeaking

Hissing

Cooing (pigeons)

I HOPE this chapter inspires your outdoor settings descriptions. The next time one of your character's steps outside, let him/her interact with or notice the wildlife within their fictional world.

19

Weather Descriptions

"WEATHER DOES PLAY a significant role in our daily lives. We might not realize it, but on some inner level, we are constantly aware of what is taking place outside. When we get dressed in the morning, we choose clothing appropriate for the outside weather. On our way out the door, we might grab a jacket or an umbrella, and perhaps our gloves. Even if we do not have a single thought about the weather before we leave the house, once outside we notice the temperature, the condition of the sky, and the presence of wind. Just as we are aware of these natural elements, so are your characters. Or at least, they should be. Their observations help ground the reader and characters in the setting and add texture to your story canvas." —*author, Larissa I. Ione*

THIS CHAPTER OFFERS fun ways to insert the weather into your settings. Weather can be a significant element when describing a setting. And certain weather conditions can undoubtedly affect people's mood. For example, a drab rainy day might make a character feel depressed or a sunny day might lift their spirits.

Weather can also become a clever plot devise if used for external conflict, such as *Man versus Nature*, or even if it forecasts (pun intended) some foreshadowing.

When depicting an outdoor scene or a character goes outside, ask yourself this: *Is it raining, cloudy, wintry, or sunshiny? Hot or cold? Damp or humid? Are the skies a clear blue or a drab grey? Is the air smoggy or fresh with the scent of rain?*

Weather can be a powerful way to enhance any setting, and incorporate atmosphere and mood. The right blend of description, introspection, climate, and action can create a strong image for the reader. A great weather description adds tension, emotion, and underlying ambiance. But poorly written descriptions can leave the reader grappling for a visual and feeling disconnected from the story. Don't forget to add the sense of *smell* to any of your outdoor scenes, and use it to make the climate or the season more realistic.

The weather can bring forth strong emotions or reactions in your characters, where the weather plays a significant role. For instance, in a Gothic tale, there would be a billowy fog, flashes of lightning, and shrieking winds. Cold, damp earthy smells and the scent of wet stone within the castle.

Descriptions of weather are most effective when it's discernible, fragrant, and tangible. Attempt to describe a hailstorm or a snowfall, an extreme heat wave, or dense twisting fog. Even a rainbow after a heavy rain in any type of genre.

Please compare these simple examples...

BLAND: It was a cold, ugly day.

REVISED: The harsh winds shook the trees as the foreboding clouds rolled in.

BLAND: It was a sunny day.

REVISED: The sun shone brightly from a clear cerulean sky.

BLAND: A storm was brewing.

REVISED: A thunderclap pealed and icy raindrops splattered the pavement.

NATURAL ELEMENTS CAN BE USED to illustrate the climate by creating a conflicting effect within an outdoor setting. For instance, a funeral can take place on a bright sunny day, or a wedding during a freak thunderstorm.

Being an avid reader, I depend on the scene's description to take me away to faraway lands and exciting locations. I love being able to step into someone else's life for a while and see it through their eyes.

Please review this descriptive writing example...

Nancy stared out the window at the dreary world outside. The faint pitter-patter of rain struck the roof. Lightning lit up the gloomy sky and winds shook the trees. She stacked more wood on the crackling flames in the fireplace to ward off the storm's chill.

I HAVE a general weather wordlist to use whenever describing the climate to use a reference tool.

Weather wordlist:

Frigid

Balmy

Warm

Pleasant

Scorcher

Sunny

Stormy

Cloudy

Tropical

Bleak

Grey

Biting

Brisk

Crisp

Dry

Harsh

Unpleasant

Icy

Clear

Cloudless

Fair

Windless

Fierce

Severe

Gale

Gusty

Humid

Muggy

Torrential

Rainy

Windy

Blizzard

Snowstorm

Cumulus

Foggy

Inclement

Mist / Misty

Nimbus

Overcast

Pall

Squall

Smog

Blazing

Fiery

Glaring

Steamy

Sticky

Dense

Sultry

Blistering

Oppressive

Shimmering Heat

Lazy Sunshine

Filtered Sunlight

Bracing

Chilly

Clammy

Damp Air

Gloomy

Dreary

Foreboding

Frosty

Icy

Arctic

Dappled Sunlight

Glacial

Bitter

Drizzle

Downpour

Thunder / Lightning

Tempestuous

Sleet

Hail

Breezy

Cool

Drizzling

Flurries

Frostbite

Rainbow

Slush / Slushy

Muddy

THIS CHAPTER SHOULD HELP to revise any scenes that incorporate the weather. Now, I challenge you to find at least three scenes in your manuscript and add a brief description of the weather to each of them.

20

Cold Weather

"...THE weather determines what we wear and how we drive, influences our experience of sporting events, field trips and beach picnics, and impacts an extraordinary number of insignificant aspects of life, such as crops and airline flights.

So, what does weather have to do with writing? Nothing. And *everything*.

Unlike much other data or information you might want in your narrative, weather is one thing you cannot simply research or vicariously live. Sure, you can watch a storm-chaser video or your favorite weather channel, but if your work is going to express any climatic realism at all, you need to get out there and experience it." —*Birgitte Rasine, author, publisher, and entrepreneur*

DESCRIBING the cold weather can add an extra layer of realism to the setting and even create a *mood* (atmospheric), or it can even tie in with your theme, or the character's emotional state.

Don't dismiss its importance to your descriptions. Weather can provide an *What are you and your character seeing, smelling, hearing, and touching?*

effective element in any type of setting. Strive to find innovative ways to *show* through a deeper POV.

When revising a scene, it's effective to imagine yourself in the actual location, and then think about the details.

Please review these simple examples...

BLAND: The weather was cold and the sky cloudy.

REVISED: Tumultuous clouds crammed the tremulous skies.

BLAND: It was a dismal afternoon and looked like it was going to rain.

REVISED: The bleak afternoon embraced grey skies and heavy clouds.

Examples of cold weather for settings:

Frost on the windows

Howling winds

Birds flying south

Heavy fog

Overcast skies

Ice on the ground

Icicles hanging from roof

Slick roads

Harsh rains

Bare trees

Somber clouds

Breath in the air

Barren Trees

I HAVE INCLUDED a wordlist to use as a reference whenever describing a colder climate.

Cold Weather Adjectives:

Below Zero

Arctic

Bare

Barren

Biting

Bitter Cold

Bleak

Blustery

Chilling

Chilly

Cloudy

Cold

Cozy

Crackling

Crisp

Crunchy

Crystalline

Dark

Dead

Depressing

Desolate

Dismal

Drafty

Dreary

Drenched

Enchanted

Extreme

Fluffy

Foggy

Freezing

Frigid

Frostbitten

Frosty

Frozen

Glacial

Glistening

Gray

Gusty

Harsh

Hazy

Howling

Hypothermic

Ice Cold

Icy

Insulated

Intensifying

Isolated

Leafless

Lonely

Melting

Misty

Nippy

Northern

Numb

Overcast

Polar

Powdery

Rainy

Severe

Shivering

Slippery

Slushy

Snowbound

Sparkling

Thaw

Windy

Wintertime

Wintery

Woolen

Zippy

SENSORY DESCRIPTIONS ARE the most essential element in any type of setting. Along with specifying certain details that pertain to the location, weather is one of the easiest ways to cement the reader in the scene and hint at the mood.

21

Warm Weather

"...THERE is the danger that comes with using the weather to mirror a character's inner emotional landscape. Mishandling this technique can quickly create melodrama. Agents and editors also say that starting with the weather may kill your chances of having your story read past the first page. Why? Because done poorly, it can sound like a weather report..." —*Angela Ackerman, co-founder of "The One Stop For Writers," an online resource that is intended to help authors improve their craft*

SOMETIMES INCLUDING the weather in the setting can be a benevolent, even a genial element, and other times Mother Nature can rage and behave like an antagonist, forcing the characters to fight for survival.

Certain types of genres require varied levels of detail when establishing the setting and world-building. For example, a high-fantasy, historical adventure, or a science fiction story will have an observant readership that expects not only graphic details and powerful imagery regarding the setting, but facts and accuracy, too.

One way to convey the weather is to have a character describe the background in his/her own "narrative voice" through the five senses, rather than using an omniscient POV.

PLEASE REVIEW THESE SIMPLE EXAMPLES...

BLAND: It was a hot, sunny day.

REVISED: The balmy breeze stroked our skin like a fiery furnace.

BLAND: The weather turned warmer.

REVISED: The sun blazed, drowning the world in a flood of golden warmth.

BLAND: The day was warm and bright.

REVISED: Bright sunlight warmed the earth.

EXAMPLES of warm weather for settings:

Wilting flowers

Brown, dead grass

Cloudless sky

Bright, hot sun

Humid

Dry winds

Sizzling concrete

Condensation on glasses

Sunburned faces or bodies

Muggy heat

Skeletal Trees

Shimmering asphalt

THIS NEXT EXCERPT is from my urban fantasy novel, "Witchy Wickedness," that depicts the weather, and also describes the character's home, neighborhood, and town.

Please review this descriptive writing example...

My parents' voices rose in pitch, bleeding out an open window. I ventured down the long, gravel driveway and stopped at the sidewalk. Overhead, a hawk flew by, a brown blur against the sky. The dull hum of bees bussing among the lavender in the neighbor's yard filled the air.

Turning my head, my gaze swept over our three-story Victorian home, squatting proudly on a hill, soft light shining through the lace-curtained windows. A rickety picket fence wrapped around the lawn and a thick row of birch trees stood like skinny sentinels along one side of the driveway, dividing the property.

I turned and walked along the sidewalk. The street appeared uninhabited, the houses strangely silent. A cool breeze ruffled the leaves, the scent of freshly cut grass, and the sun peeking through the clouds cast a warm, safe glow over everything. In other towns, this would have been a pleasant suburb.

Except this was Ravenwood, evil's favorite haunting grounds. Like other coastal areas, Ravenwood seemed serene among the lush landscape during the day—except after nightfall, people locked their doors and kept their children inside. It was as if the community realized long ago that the divider between our world and the supernatural realm was gossamer-thin.

I HAVE INCLUDED a glossary to use as a reference whenever describing a warmer environment.

Warm Weather Adjectives:

Ablaze

Air-Conditioned

Balmy

Blazing

Blistering

Boiling

Breezy

Bright

Burning

Clammy

Clear

Cloudless

Endless

Fragrant

Green

Hazy

Sweltering

Humid

Oppressive

Ripe

Roasting

Scorching

Sizzling

Steamy

Sticky

Sultry

Summery

Sun-Drenched

Sunburnt

Sunny

Sweaty

Stifling

Toasty

Tan skin

Tropical

Warm

I WANT to encourage every writer that reads this guide to include a sentence or two about the weather in any outdoor scenes.

22

Mood / Atmosphere

"SETTING ISN'T the same as atmosphere, but it is a big part of it and can help to shape the mood of the story. A story set in an abandoned warehouse immediately evokes a sense of eeriness and isolation, of neglect and dreariness. Make sure you choose a setting, which suits the type of story you're writing. Different settings create different atmospheres. In a ghost story, you want the atmosphere to be creepy and one of trepidation. An ideal setting is an old theatre or graveyard. A setting on a crowded beach in Malaga induces a very different atmosphere." —*Esther Newton, writer and tutor for The Writers Bureau*

THIS CHAPTER WILL FOCUS on how adding a dash of evocative atmosphere (mood) to your settings. The location itself can create a strong emotional ambiance, and it can even hint at the theme in your story. One way to do that is to incorporate the five senses through descriptive writing.

However, I would avoid describing the setting with a cliché. Consider the setting not only as a factual location, but also as a crucial part of a story's ambiance to give each scene greater impact. Vibrant settings can establish a distinct *mood* within any type of genre. For instance, in a gothic narrative, a writer could describe a fog shrouded castle and instantly transport the reader into their eerie fictional world.

Please review this descriptive writing example...

The room pulsated with dark energy, as if it were alive, breathing and writhing in pain. Or maybe it was mirroring my own tumbling emotions. Beneath my feet, the hardwood floor grumbled with power, like a sleeping beast. The loud furnace roared, as though it were the house's beating heart. Ghostly moans echoed throughout the corridor and a chill draft swept over my skin.

THAT EXAMPLE SHOULD GIVE you an idea on how writing description by using atmosphere and the five senses can create a vivid scene.

Reference wordlist to describe atmosphere and mood:

Abandoned

Alienated

Benevolent

Blithe

Calm

Casual

Comforting

Delightful

Earnest

Effusive

Empathetic

Euphoric

Facetious

Fervent

Light

Modest

Nostalgic

Placid

Direct

Impartial

Indirect

Unambiguous

Understated

Poignant

Proud

Relaxed

Reverent

Romantic

Sanguine

Scholarly

Sentimental

Serene

Silly

Sprightly

Straightforward

Tranquil

Whimsical

Wistful

Worshipful

Zealous

Abhorring

Acerbic

Ambiguous

Ambivalent

Bitter

Blunt

Cold

Desolate

Despairing

Desperate

Detached

Evasive

Forceful

Foreboding

Gloomy

Grave

Grim

Harsh

Haughty

Melancholy

Miserable

Mocking

Mournful

Ominous

Pathetic

Pensive

Pretentious

Resigned

Reticent

Severe

Sinister

Solemn

Somber

Stern

Stolid

Strident

Threatening

Tragic

Uneasy

Unfriendly

Unsympathetic

Violent

Wry

THIS INFORMATIVE CHAPTER on including a sense of "mood" in the setting should inspire you to revise your own setting descriptions.

23

Nighttime Description

"REFERENCES TO TIME and day (or month or season or year) are necessary to keep readers linked with story events and hold them deep inside the fiction. Without enough time markers, readers may be confused and find themselves turning back to earlier pages to try to figure out when they are in that story..." —*Beth Hill, freelance fiction editor*

AS A FICTION WRITER, you are the artist and landscaper doing the world-building within your reader's imagination. Be inspired to welcome the magnificence of description by applying dramatic attention to every detail in your individual settings.

To avoid doing a description info-dump, aim to blend elements regarding the location by lacing the setting's details throughout the dialogue and action. By including the time of day in a scene, it will help to convey the passing of time or reveal the time of day, too.

PLEASE REVIEW THESE SIMPLE EXAMPLES...

BLAND: The sunset looked golden.

REVISED: As the sun set, the hillside turned a shimmering gold.

BLAND: A big moon hung over the neighborhood.

REVISED: The full moon bathed the neighborhood in a luminous glow.

BLAND: I saw the sky darken and fill with clouds.

REVISED: Wispy clouds drifted lazily across the night sky.

BLAND: The night was cold and dark.

REVISED: A chill, night wind howled through the oaks and made the branches shiver.

I'll admit that not all of my revisions are very original, but they are definitely an improvement on the blander sentences that state the facts in a dull and telling way.

LIST of general times and moons:

Evening

Nightfall

Sundown

Late afternoon

Midnight

Dusk

Twilight

Dinner

Sunset

Full Moon

Crescent Moon

WORDLIST REFERENCE TO DESCRIBE NIGHT, *nighttime, or even darkness:*

Caliginosity

Darkness

Dead of Night

Dimness

Evening

Gloom

Murkiness

Gloaming

Nightfall

Nighttime

Obscurity

Opacity

Semidarkness

Shade

Shadows

Twilight

Cimmerian

Aphotic

Caliginous

Clouded / Cloudy

Crepuscular

Dingy

Dusk / Dusky

Faint

Foggy

Indistinct

Inky

Misty

Murky

Nebulous

Eclipse

Obscure

Opaque

Overcast

Darkness

Pitchy

Rayless

Shaded

Shadowy

Somber

Sooty

Stygian

Sunless

Obscure

Vague

Gloaming

Lugubrious

Nyctophobia

Nocturnal

WORDS AND PHRASES with powerful sensory connotations always increase the chances of producing an empathic response in the reader.

24

Daytime Descriptions

"WE GIVE characters individual voices to make them feel real, so that the cast members of our novels don't feel like two-dimensional carbon copies of each other. Just like a character, a place in your story should have its own 'voice'. Write place like you would write a character..." —*Bridget McNulty, author, content strategist, editor, and speaker*

Whether you're crafting a short story, fanfiction, or an epic historical adventure, fictional moments pass just like real time passes. It's important to mention the passing of time in your narrative whenever the story jumps forward in time or a there's a new scene.

To avoid plot holes in your timeline of events, it might help to include time-markers. Strive to include the time of day whenever a new scene takes place or there's a new chapter to let the reader know how much time has passed.

PLEASE REVIEW THESE SIMPLE EXAMPLES...

BLAND: The morning sun rose on the hillside.

REVISED: The sun rose, staining the hillside in shades of crimson and gold.

BLAND: It was afternoon on a cloudy day.

REVISED: The afternoon clouds crowded the grey skies.

BLAND: That afternoon, it felt cold and dreary.

REVISED: The afternoon sky was burdened with dreary clouds.

LIST OF GENERAL TIMES:

Sunup

Daybreak

Morning

Daylight

Afternoon

Dawn

Breakfast

Brunch

Lunch

Sunrise

WORDLIST TO DESCRIBE daytime or sunshine:

Sunny

Resplendent

Bright

Intense

Unclouded

Burnished

Ablaze

Actinic

Cloudless

Abundant

Blinding

Bright

Dappled

Dazzling

Diffused

Filtered

Glaring

Glorious

Golden

Hazy

Indirect

Intense

Mellow

Streaming

Gleaming

Glimmering

Glinting

Glittering

Illuminating

Incandescent

Iridescent

Lucent

Luminescent / Luminous

Lustrous

Opalescent

Penumbral

Phosphorescent

Prismatic

Radiant

Resplendent

Dazzling

Shimmering

I\u1d1b's easy in early drafts to depend on simple, straightforward descriptions of the setting without mentioning the time of day.

25

Seasonal Descriptions

"W‌HEN WE TALK about story settings, seasons are often underused. Even if you live somewhere like me where you get to experience all four of them, you might still need tips for using seasons in writing. Story setting can almost be like a character by itself, but our environment is one of those things that we kind of tend to take for granted..." —*Katri Soikkeli, author and creative business owner*

W‌HEN DESCRIBING locations within your marvelous fictional world, it's a good idea to include a mention of the season. Each season is distinctive, and it not only affects the weather and nature herself, but it also signals important events during our calendar year. Consider the weather, province, and holidays within the timeline of your story.

To cement readers into any fictional world, show them a man delivering newspapers or garbage cans lined up by the curb. Let the reader *see, hear,* and *touch* your scenes. Don't let characters float around in space—firmly attach them to the setting.

Each new scene needs to establish where the characters are or your readers cannot visualize the setting or where the scene takes place. One way to do that is to include a mention of the seasons.

The main four seasons are: Summer, Fall, Winter, and Spring.

There are lots of ways to include the seasons in your own work, and these examples should be inspiring.

Please review these simple examples...

BLAND: When I walked outside, I smelled pine from the trees.

REVISED: The essence of pine floated on the autumn winds.

BLAND: It was springtime and flowers were everywhere on the hillside.

REVISED: The rural hillside was covered in spring's flourish of poppies.

HERE IS an excerpt from one of my cozy mystery novels that describes the weather, season, and setting.

Please review this descriptive writing example...

Tricksy and I got into the Mazda convertible and drove to Bewitching Books. It was a beautiful spring afternoon, with the birds chirping and the scent of honeysuckle on the wind. A few tourists were meandering along the sidewalks in the downtown area studded with antique shops, cafés, bakeries, and funky art galleries. I'd really come to adore Hemlock Hills nestled into a rustic landscape and bordering a national seashore. The day seemed so serene, no one would ever believe that two women had recently been bludgeoned to death in this idyllic community.

I HAVE INCLUDED a directory of different holidays that might affect your story's setting or timeline.

Wordlist of holidays to consider depending on the season:

Valentine's Day

Easter

Mother's Day

Father's Day

Halloween

Thanksgiving

Christmas

Hanukkah

New Year's Day

Memorial Day

Independence Day

Labor Day

St. Patrick's Day

Chanukah/Hanukkah

April Fool's Day

Good Friday

Veterans Day

Fourth of July

Please review these simple holiday related examples...

BLAND: Halloween was finally here and we had lots of trick-or-treaters.

REVISED: The trick-or-treaters shrieked and giggled on the porch as they waited for me to open the door with candy.

BLAND: It was Thanksgiving and I'd prepared to make the meal.

REVISED: The scents of cinnamon, cloves, and margarine wafted in the kitchen as I prepared the Thanksgiving meal.

BLAND: The school gym had been decorated for Valentine's Day.

REVISED: Pink paper hearts fluttered in the air-conditioned breeze of the gymnasium.

PLEASE KEEP in mind while you're rewriting certain scenes in your fictional tale to ensure that the timeline accurately conveys the seasons, any celebrations, and holidays.

26

Seasonal Scents

"I LOVE the rewriting and redrafting process. Once I have a first draft, I print the whole thing out and do the first pass with handwritten notes. I write all kinds of notes in the margins and scribble and cross things out. I note down new scenes that need writing, continuity issues, problems with characters and much more. That first pass usually takes a while. Then I go back and start a major rewrite based on those notes..." —*Joanna Penn, The Creative Penn blog*

FICTIONAL WORLDS DO NOT EXIST until you acutely describe them on the page. Creative and imaginative descriptions gives the writing a sense of originality and believability, while nondescript details can make the prose seem vague and implausible.

Just remember as your drafting your next masterpiece, the settings should serve a purpose, and not just pad the writing with more words. Sensory details can create concrete images, and they should relate to one or more of the five senses. Many of them can be adjectives, although they can also function as verbs or adverbs, depending on how they are used in a sentence.

The setting is often an afterthought by most writers, but it can have a huge influence and effect on your story. The descriptions of locations, backdrops, or landscapes can even function like an actual character that impacts the plot and emotions of your characters.

I HAVE AN INCLUDED a bonus section of descriptive words from my own personal "scent/smell" database that I've found useful for creating stronger scenes. Please include these wordlists as a powerful reference tool in your own writer's toolbox!

Christmas / Winter scents:

Pinecones, Fresh-Baked Gingerbread, Mulled Wine, Apple Cider, Fig Pudding, Cranberry, Nutmeg, Cinnamon, French Vanilla, Butter, Baked Ham, Woodsmoke, Bayberry Candles, Orange and Cloves, Peppermint, Roasted Chestnuts, Brown Sugar, Gingerbread, Hot Chocolate, Evergreen, Eggnog, Wet Cedar, Wet Woolen Mittens, Bread Rising And Baking, A Pot of Coffee, Frying Bacon, Spruce Needles, Sage And Thyme, Crisp Smell of Fresh Snow.

Springtime scents:

Lilacs In Bloom, Insect Repellent Spray, Suntan Lotion, Corn On The Cob, Watermelon, Cantaloupe, New Hay, Petunias, Charcoal Starter, Seashore, Salty Ocean Breeze, Chlorine, Blueberry Muffin, Gasoline, Campfires, Lavender, Freshly Cut Grass, Fresh Laundry, Cherries, Melon, Ripe Red Strawberries, Cucumber, Shaving Cream, Talc Powder, Sandalwood.

Summer / Warm Weather scents:

Honey-Suckle, sea drifting inland on the wind, Orange Ice-Cream Bars, Tangerine, Licorice, Bubble Gum, Lemonade, Iced Tea, Perspiration, Cola – Soda, Sea Salt, Fishy, Seaweed or Algae, Coconut Oil, BBQ Sauce, Bamboo, Fresh Sliced Pineapple, Downy April Fresh Fabric Softener, Fragrant Teak Wood, Clean Scent of Cotton, Powdery Musk, Exhaust Fumes, Juniper Bushes, Freshly Cut Flowers, Honey, Inflatable Plastic.

Halloween / Back to School scents:

Jack-O-Lantern Innards, Candy, Chocolate, Hot Glue, Cornstalks, Damp Leaves, Overturned Earth, Rotting Brown Apples, Roasting Pumpkin Seeds, Chili, Cornbread, Cinnamon, Nutmeg, Tea, Potpourri, Smoking Match, Rain-Soaked Leaves, Distant Fires, Hay, Unpolluted Pure Scent of Rain, Leather, Pencil Lead/Graphite, Dried Corn Kernels Cooking, Wet Dog, Moss, Rotten Wood, Decaying Leaves, Buttery Popcorn, Cotton Candy.

Thanksgiving / Autumn scents:

Cedar Wood, Bay Rum, Turkey, Scalloped Potatoes, Pecan Pie, Pumpkin Pie, Homemade Rolls, Walnut, Banana Nut Bread, Cranberry Spice, Green and Musky Scent of Bergamot, key, Scalloped Potatoes, Pecan Pie, Pumpkin Pie, Homemade Rolls, Walnut, Banana Nut Bread, Cranberry Spice, Green and Coffee Cake.

WHEN YOU USE descriptive writing and activate the five senses within your reader or arouse their emotions, then you are creating an engrossing and entertaining read.

Now I encourage you to go through your own manuscripts and revise your scenes into dramatic and realistic settings.

In the following chapters, I will share methods that you can use to imaginatively describe your characters in easy and fun ways that will instantly inspire your creative muse.

27

Character Descriptions

"THE DESCRIPTION of a new character who has just entered your story having "big brown eyes and frizzy black hair" or "ginger hair that cascaded down her shoulders and eyes the color of jade." *Really*—does stating a woman has brown eyes and frizzy black hair give a reader ANY sense of what she looks like? Does it reveal anything unique about her that doesn't apply to 500,000 other people? Does it reveal anything about her character? Nay, nay and nay." —*Meghan Ward, author, freelance writer and blogger*

CHARACTER DEPICTIONS ARE MUCH MORE imaginative, lifelike, and visual for readers when a character has intriguing physical qualities and distinctive, memorable features.

This chapter focuses on ways that you can describe a character's physical appearance though descriptive writing. While some of you may prefer minimal character descriptions because you'd rather the reader imagine a character's appearance in their own way, I feel that *some* description of your characters is vital to good storytelling. And too little description can cause reader confusion.

For instance, have you ever read a book and visualized the main character as a lanky, brown-haired older man, only to discover fifty pages into the story that the character was a brawny, tan, blond younger man? It's jarring to the reader and can create a negative response.

Whenever a new character is introduced, I recommend including a brief description, but avoid giving the reader a boring grocery list of attributes.

Please compare these simple examples...

BLAND: Camryn had brown hair and a freckled skin. She had gray eyes and a birthmark under her right eye that I noticed when she smiled.

While the first example states the facts and describes the character, it's painfully boring, isn't it? Let's see if I can revise this bland description.

REVISED: Camryn's generous mouth lifted into a friendly smile, making her gray eyes crinkle at the corners. Her shaggy brown hair framed a freckled face, and a slight birthmark under her right eye stained her pale cheekbone.

The second version is an improvement when compared to the first example. Let's consider more ways you can apply descriptive writing.

WHENEVER DEPICTING A CHARACTER, only choose the details that form the clearest, most informative impact. One or two relevant details like clothing or a distinct feature, like a mole, scar, or broken nose. Another way to depict a character is to focus on distinctive characteristics that highlight their unique personality, such as biting their fingernails, a wandering eye, or a nervous twitch.

A word of caution: avoid an info-dump of character description that slows the pace. There's no need to overload the scene with too many physical descriptions or disclose all of a character's personality traits in the same scene.

THROUGHOUT THIS GUIDE, I have provided excerpts from my own fiction writing to illustrate how descriptive writing can enhance a scene that I hope you will find encouraging.

Here is a passage from my adult urban fantasy novel, "Shadow Magic," that describes both the setting and the characters, and weaves in a first-person POV character's clothing description.

Please review this descriptive writing example...

Ms. Lore had a cramped office with dilapidated blinds on a lone window. The small space had wood-paneled walls and one side was lined with bookcases holding leather-bound tomes on dusty shelves. A ceramic pot of pink geraniums huddled in the corner and brightened the drab room with a splash of color.

"Most students who enroll at Macabre after attending other colleges find it to be a difficult adjustment. Advanced courses can be grueling." Ms. Lore peered over the rim of her glasses. "Though your grades are spectacular, this college had a last-minute opening, which is the only reason why Dean Witchbane accepted your registration."

My advisor, an elf with a greenish complexion, had wedged her pudgy body between the chair and the oversized desk that was situated over a shabby rug. Her lily-of-the-valley perfume overrode the stench of onions from the half-eaten bagel sitting atop a book titled: *How to Train Your Familiar.*

I forced a grin. "Then I'll be sure to bring my A-game."

She stirred her chai tea, the spoon clanging against the sides of the porcelain cup. Ms. Lore's round face reminded me of a chipmunk, and her pointy ears poked out of her chestnut-brown hair that brushed her shoulders. "You are lucky to be here, Miss LeStrange. Macabre University is one of the finest institutions in the world."

"And don't I know it." I unbuttoned the kelly-green military jacket I'd worn over a white tank-top, with a light-green scarf and distressed, skinny jeans. I crossed my legs, swinging a black ankle boot.

ONE WAY TO describe a character is to start with the head-to-toe method. Start off by describing the upper part of the body, like the face and head, and then continue downward until you get to the legs or feet. Strive to weave in only the features that will give the reader the most effective visual, such as mentioning the hairstyle and color, then the eye shape and color, followed by any distinguishing facial features.

Whenever describing a character, ask yourself: What sets this character apart from the other characters in my narrative?

For instance: *Does the character have freckles? A dimpled chin? Moles? A missing eye? Scars? Birthmarks? Crooked teeth? A strong schnoz? Round, flush cheeks? Cute dimples? A wide Joker-smile? Big forehead? High-cheekbones? Thin lips?*

When you finish the facial description, then you can move onto the chest and arms, and perhaps the height and weight, too. The description doesn't need to overly detailed. Having more than a page of character description is unnecessary, and might bore the reader. If you want your character description to be effective and memorable, it's a good idea to strive to make it as unique as possible.

I have included another excerpt from my adult urban fantasy novel, "Shadow Magic," which describes a character's features in a fun and unique way.

Please review this descriptive writing example...

Professor Mortis scrutinized the room, his piercing stare slashing at our confidence. His tall, lanky frame towered over most of the students, and his pallid complexion resembled the underbelly of a dying fish. He'd styled his dark hair in a severe side-part, and he wore a brown oxford shirt and slacks under a black lab coat.

WHEN DESCRIBING a character's physical appearance, sometimes detailed facts about their features, such as height and weight, are usually not quite visual enough.

You need to make all of your characters as three-dimensional as possible, so that the reader sees them as real people. One way to do that is to use descriptive writing, but choose your words carefully, because they will reveal a lot about your characters.

PLEASE COMPARE THIS SIMPLE EXAMPLE...

BLAND: Cyrus was standing on the other side of the dining room, greeting his dinner guests. He looked unremarkable—bald, fat, and he wore an outdated blue suit. He had food in his thick mustache.

When he removed his jacket, there were sweat marks on the underarms of his shirt.

That is a rather bland, yawn-inducing description. Let me see if I can better convey the same information through descriptive writing and narrative "voice."

REVISED: Cyrus stood on the other side of the dining room, greeting his dinner guests. His baldhead shone under the glow of the chandelier, and a piece of brie was wedged in his untrimmed mustache.

When he waddled around the oak table, his stomach jiggled like a jolly Santa, barely hidden behind a blue double-breasted suit. When he shrugged off his jacket, sweat marks stained his underarms.

The revision is an improvement and gives the reader a more dramatic visual of the character.

I HOPE that you find the excerpts and examples in this chapter inspirational.

A word of caution: be careful of mentioning a physical trait more than two or three times within the narrative because then the reader will think it has some importance to the plot, and if it doesn't, then there is no need to mention it multiple times. If you describe a character's freckled skin, only do it once or twice at most. In an early draft of one of my novels, I stated that the heroine had a belly-ring at least four or five times whenever I was describing her clothing. A reviewer made a nasty comment about it being overkill...and, well, it was. I removed almost every mention of it and focused more on her ugly scar, which did have a significant connection to the plot.

Now, I encourage you to revise any character descriptions in your own stories through "narrative voice" and descriptive writing.

28

Physical Attributes

"THE CHARACTERS IN OUR STORIES, songs, poems, and essays embody our writing. They are our words made flesh. Sometimes they even speak for us, carrying much of the burden of plot, theme, mood, idea, and emotion. But they do not exist until we describe them on the page. Until we anchor them with words, they drift, bodiless and ethereal. They weigh nothing; they have no voice."—*excerpt from "Word Painting" by Rebecca McClanahan*

STRIVE to make all of your characters three-dimensional. When you describe a character, it's important to be as descriptive as possible without making it read like an inventory of attributes. Don't just tell the reader that John was handsome or that Jane was overweight, but try to *show* it through descriptive writing.

Possible physical attributes might be:

Face: bleak, bony, emaciated, fleshy, round, rough, chiseled, angular, delicate, oval, feminine, arresting, masculine, square, oblong, heart-shaped, broad forehead, sharp cheekbones, hollow cheeks, sculpted, craggy, jowly

Nose: long, big nostrils, crooked, hook, bulbous, pointy, upturned, aquiline, refined, aristocratic, defined, Romanesque, dainty, broad, crooked, strong

Lips: thin, colorless, uneven, cracked, dry, flat, plump, sensual, firm, full, glossy, narrow, rosebud, chapped, overbite

Eyes: beady, squinty, bloodshot, dull, hooded, rheumy, sunken, cat-shaped, exotic, dreamy, expressive, doe-eyed, brilliant, narrow, sharp, squinty, wide-set, close-set, deep-set, bulging, protruding, hooded, glassy, heavy-lidded, flecked, dull, bleary, cloudy, red-rimmed, beady, steely

Hair: tangled, unwashed, unevenly cut, frizzy, bouncy, shiny, silky, flowing, thick, velvety, soft, curly, dull, flat, limp, straggly, thin, thick, coarse

Ears: pointy, small, large, droopy, floppy, stick-out, small, flat, cute, curving

Chin: protruding, pointy, double-chin, angular, chiseled, square, cleft

Complexion: wrinkly, acne, stretch marks, scars, warts, rough, veiny, porcelain, bronzed, flawless, smooth, supple, rugged

Teeth: crooked, missing teeth, pointy, large, chipped, overbite, yellow, white, straight, pearly, toothy, perfect

Eyebrows: bushy, heavy, thick, shaggy, thin, amber, arched, lifted, raised, waxed, plucked, shaped, sparse, unruly, prominent brow

Skin color: orangey, tawny, tan, bronze, dark-brown, mocha brown, ebony, caramel, honey, golden-brown, insipid, pallid, pasty, fair, alabaster, ivory, milky-white, porcelain, chalky, sallow, olive, peach, ruddy, sunburnt, red, bleached

Facial hair: clean-shaven, beard, goatee, grizzly, smooth-shaven, moustache, sideburns, bushy, thick, stubble, growth, whiskers, five o'clock shadow, scruffy

Body types: tall, short, petite, compact, bulky, large, big-boned, husky, beefy, brawny, heavy / heavy-set, flabby, chunky, chubby, pudgy, stout, stocky, thick, full-figured, voluptuous, curvy, overweight, flabby, puny, weak, boney, meaty, slender, athletic, muscular, lithe, buffed, scrawny, big-boned, curvy, hourglass figure, plump, gangling, lanky, willowy, svelte, lean, slim, thin, pear-shaped, skinny, emaciated, gaunt, wiry, rangy, sinewy, hulking, toned, taut, ripped, broad-shouldered

MAKE every effort to describe characters as they are introduced into the storyline, and as early as possible. With descriptive writing, you can skillfully tuck the physical characteristics of your characters into the narrative through action and dialogue.

The best technique to describing characters is to present just enough relevant details to help your reader instantly "see" the character in their mind, with the right blend of description and introspection.

When describing characters weave in descriptions of their clothing, age, hair and eye color, height, weight, visible scars, and even nationality, etc. into the scene.

Please compare these simple examples...

BLAND: Cole leaned against the car wearing tan pants. He had blond hair and blue eyes. And when his full lips grinned at me, I realized that I really liked him.

While that example portrays the character, it's not very descriptive or has any narrative "voice." Let's see if I can improve it in the revision.

REVISED: Cole stuffed his hands into the pockets of his wrinkled khakis as he reclined his large frame against the black Mustang. The breeze ruffled his blond hair, and I yearned to brush the golden strands from his cerulean eyes. When those generous lips tipped into an arrogant grin, I knew my heart was in big trouble.

I think that you'll agree that the second example is more interesting and descriptive than the first one. Let's review a few more illustrations.

Please compare these simple examples...

BLAND: Brock had black hair and thin features. His blue eyes stood out against his tan skin and large nose. I admired his tall, sturdy-looking body.

REVISED: Brock's glossy black hair framed his narrow face. His clear blue eyes stood out in contrast to his tan skin, which had the look of a man who spent a lot of time outdoors. Brock rubbed his bold nose as he ducked under the doorway to enter the room, his robust body lumbering forward like a gentle giant.

I REALIZE that most of my revision examples aren't terribly original, but they should still give you a clearer understanding on ways to rewrite any bland, filtered descriptions into a stronger visual for your readers. Again, using a filter word on occasion is perfectly okay when needed and always acceptable in dialogue.

To better clarify my point, I have included an excerpt from my adult cozy paranormal mystery novel, "Booked For Murder," which depicts a character through descriptive writing, "voice," the senses, and emotional reactions.

Please review this descriptive writing example...

We waited near the desk, the aroma of vanilla coffee wafting throughout the lobby.

The man reading the magazine raised his head, and my lips parted on a soft inhale. He was in his mid-thirties, with cobalt blue eyes and a scruffy, gorgeousness that I found irresistibly attractive. His long, jean-clad legs were stretched out in front of him and his light-brown hair was brushed off his face. He lowered his head and scratched above his rather pointy ear. If I had to guess based on his looks and woodsy scent, his pedigree was werewolf.

Werewolves could shift into a wolf anytime they wanted, and they retained their human intelligence while transformed and their wolf senses while in human form. Most werewolves were a bit on the hairy side, had deep voices, superior senses, and regenerative powers. They were nothing like the aggressive carnivores portrayed in books and movies, and most were vegetarians.

I drew in a shaky breath. Could this be Vaughn Wulfstein?

HERE IS an excerpt from my adult urban fantasy novel. "Shadow Magic," that describes a character.

Please review this descriptive writing example...

He was at least five-foot-nine, and unconventionally attractive. The lamplight fell across his face highlighting a strong nose, slanted green eyes, and a paintbrush flick of freckles dotting his cheeks. His pale skin had noticeable light-blue veins and his eyes appeared bloodshot. The handsome vampire wore faded jeans with a black, short-sleeved, V-neck shirt that molded to his muscular body.

THE FOLLOWING passage was also from my adult urban fantasy novel to provide you with another illustration on describing characters in a deeper POV, along with a first-person narrator.

Please review this descriptive writing example...

Feeling hot and prickly, despite the chill in the room, I unbuttoned my lab coat. Professor Mortis droned on about necroplasm, but I barely listened. I caught sight of the other students' distorted reflections in the glass cabinets above a stainless-steel counter. Everyone looked humanoid in appearance, and normally all necromancers had black hair and bright-green flecks in their eyes, yet I had one glaring difference. I was born with vivid blue hair, making me resemble Cookie Monster's love child. Once I'd wasted a thousand dollars on an elfin glamour to conceal the bright strands, but it dissolved within an hour.

And contrary to popular belief, necromancers didn't wear black tunics and hang out in graveyards. Personally, I always made an effort to look fashion-fierce, and today, I'd worn a black V-neck shirt with a jean mini-skirt and Jimmy Choo biker boots beneath my lab coat.

IF YOU SPRINKLE physical characteristics into a scene mixed with the action, dialogue, and introspection, it will instantly enrich the reader's experience.

29

Hair Descriptions

"INTRODUCING a new character to your story can be difficult. There's a lot that goes into it, and to make matters worse, you only have one chance to give readers a good (and memorable) first impression of that character. One of the ways you can do this is by giving them a distinct appearance, but many writers tend to fall short of describing appearance well..." *Jules, artist, writer, editor, and blogger of All Write Alright*

THIS CHAPTER FOCUSES on ways to describe a character's hair. Adding descriptions of hair can add an extra layer of realism to your characters. If you write young adult fiction, remember that teens often express themselves through fashion and hairstyles.

Powerful character descriptions can add flair to your scenes, and create a sense of intimacy between your characters and readers. I recommend describing your character's hair in fun and imaginative ways, and not just stating it blandly for the reader.

Please review these simple examples...

FILTERED: She had red hair.

REVISED: Her crimson highlights shone in the sunlight.

HAIR IS JUST another form of expression for most people, even fictional characters. Do research on current trends and hair colors, or if your story is about a snobby, affluent family, try adding descriptive words about their flawlessly coiffed hairstyles.

As an illustration, I have included two short excerpts from my urban fantasy novel, "Demon Dreadful," that depicts a character description.

Please review these two descriptive writing examples...

A moment later, a fiftyish year-old Hispanic man with salt and pepper hair entered, wearing a sweeping black coat. His presence raised the hairs along the nape of my neck. He was about five-foot eight, with a stout frame and dark-brown eyes. He approached and laid a warm hand on my arm. My muscles went rigid beneath his calloused fingers.

HER STRAWBERRY-BLONDE HAIR hung in spirals past her shoulders and she wore all black: turtleneck, pants, and sneakers, like a female spy. Her sparkling eyes and smile were as bright as sunshine on a cloudy day.

HERE IS one more excerpt from my YA urban fantasy novel, "Slayers & Spells," that describes a character's features, hair, and clothing style.

Please review this descriptive writing example...

The side-gate scraped open and shut. Cryptic Boy walked over. He'd help me scare off these no-face demons one night and he showed up on occasion with warnings, which were actually helpful, but I always failed to get his real name.

Peering closer, I noticed a small Y-shaped scar on his left eyebrow and I guessed he was about eighteen or nineteen. Cryptic Boy wore a black duster over faded jeans, a T-shirt, and combat boots, making him resemble a scruffy, rockstar. His midnight hair grazed his slim shoulders, creating a perfect frame for his chiseled features. His violet-blue stare held mine, and a warm, outdoorsy scent like campfires wafted in the air around him.

The boy nudged loose hair from his eyes with a cool, macho guy flick of his head. "Hey."

NOW, let's discuss different hair types that encompass all racial and ethnic races that you can use to describe a character's flowing mane. Instead of just stating that a character's hair looked wavy or straight or curly, I suggest being more inventive with your depictions.

Human hair has diverse types and textures. Hairstyles differ extensively across various cultures, and it's often used to signify a person's social status or personality, and it can also convey their age, gender, ethnic background, and religion.

According to most cosmetologists there are only three types of hair:

AFRICAN

African-Americans usually have tight curls, thick hair, and the color is a natural dark brown or black.

ASIAN

Asian hair is usually straight and thick and shiny. It contrasts in colors from deep black to medium brown.

CAUCASIAN (EUROPEAN)

Caucasian or European hair can be straight, wavy, or curly. It fluctuates in color from dark brown to flaxen. This hair type can be either fine, medium, or coarse.

PLEASE COMPARE THESE SIMPLE EXAMPLES…

BLAND: She had blonde curly hair.

While it states a fact and describes the character's hair, it's a dull description. Let's see if I can enhance this depiction.

REVISED: She shook her flaxen head, the coiled strands bouncing on her shoulders.

My revision is much more visual when compared to the first example. Let's review a few more examples.

Here is a short excerpt from my science fiction romance novel that describes a first-person POV character's looks and hair.

Please review this descriptive writing example...

I catch my reflection in the glass doors of the china cabinet behind him. My hazel eyes are red and watery, with dark smudges of mascara staining my pale face. My purple and black colored waves look disheveled, and I ran a hand through the tangled strands.

MAKE sure that the hair descriptors you choose fit the character and their ethnic background. I have included a list of hair textures in this chapter to inspire your creativity.

Thesaurus of hair textures:

Bald patches

Balding

Bleached

Dry

Limp

Oily

Fine

Course

Straight

Corkscrew Curls

Curly

Nappy

Wavy

Thin / Fine

Frizzy

Thick

Wooly

Greasy

Brittle

Chemically damaged

Dandruff

Hair loss / horseshoe

Ringlets

Spirals

Bouncy

Wispy

Stringy

Straggly

Tangled

Windblown

THIS CHAPTER SHOULD ENCOURAGE you to skillfully describe a character's hairstyle and other features.

30

Hairstyles

A CHARACTER'S hairstyle will convey a lot about their personality. Most of us believe that we should *never* judge a book by its cover, but we all still do it on some sub-conscience level.

A character's description is like first meeting someone and assessing their lifestyle, personality, and background.

Hairstyles from wild to conventional, or trendy to outdated, tells the reader a lot about a character's social class, personal style, and personality.

For instance, a former beauty pageant queen who visits the salon every Saturday morning to get her hair styled might be considered a pampered diva. Or a young man who only goes to the barber every six months to get a haircut might be considered less concerned about his appearance. If the character has a short, wash-and-go style, they might be a no-nonsense type of personality. It most likely means they don't want to fuss over things in life, including their hair because they're sporty or outdoorsy. And characters with longer hair-styles might be more concerned with their looks.

Get to know your characters by answering these questions:
How much time does the character spend on their hair each morning?
How often do they change their hairstyle?
Does the character color their hair?
What's their bad hair day solution?
How important is their hair to them on a scale from 1-10?

PLEASE COMPARE THESE SIMPLE EXAMPLES…

BLAND: I saw my ex-boyfriend had a stylish haircut that looked sexy.

While it describes the character's hairstyle, it's too nondescript in my opinion. Let's see if I can enrich this description.

REVISED: My ex had trendy hair tapered in the back and across both sides, but left heavy on top in a sexy mess.

I feel it's a much better depiction when compared to the first example.

I HAVE INCLUDED a list of hairstyles as inspiration whenever describing your characters.

Thesaurus list of hairstyles:

Blow-dry

Braided

Classic Bob

Crown Braids

Curly

Elegant updo

Short and Spiky

Fringe

Pompadour

Blunt

Bangs

Wavy

Wedding Hair

Ponytail

Afro

Beehive

Bouffant

Braided

Ballerina-Bun

Buzzed

Chignon

Comb-Over

Cornrows

Crew Cut

Dreadlocks

Fauxhawk / Mohawk

Finger-waves

Flattop

Fade

Spikes

Feathered

Mullet

HERE'S an additional list of hair descriptors to use when portraying your characters to use as a reference.

Wordlist of hair descriptors:

Bobbed

Bushy

Close-Cropped

Crinkly

Curtained

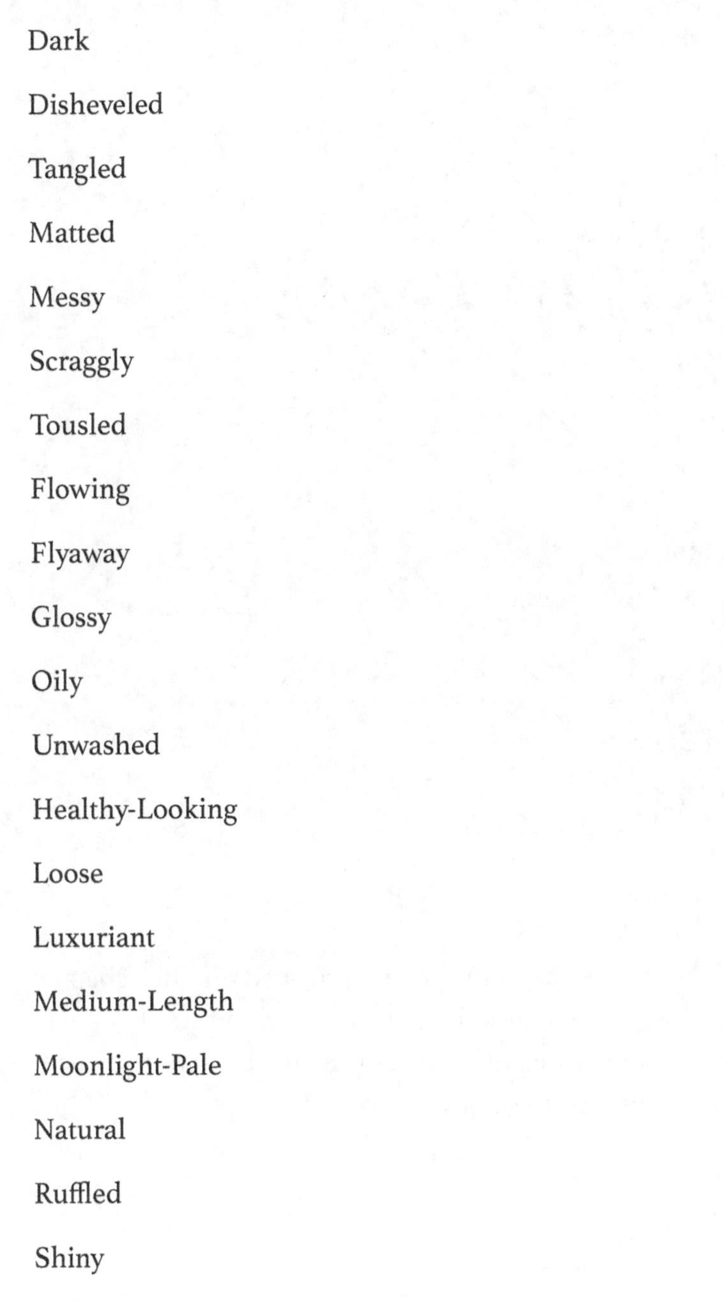

Damp

Dark

Disheveled

Tangled

Matted

Messy

Scraggly

Tousled

Flowing

Flyaway

Glossy

Oily

Unwashed

Healthy-Looking

Loose

Luxuriant

Medium-Length

Moonlight-Pale

Natural

Ruffled

Shiny

Short

Shoulder-Length

Silky

Sleek

Slicked

Spiky

Straight

Thick

Thin

Thinning

Wavy

Well-Kept

Wind-Blown

Windswept

THE LISTS and the information provided in this chapter should help when describing a character's outward appearance. I hope this chapter encourages you to craft realistic hair descriptions in your own narratives.

31

Hair Colors

"IN AN EFFORT TO dodge the "show, don't tell" bullet, a lot of writers have taken the external route in conveying the emotions of their character. As I've said before, there's Bad Telling, and there's Good Telling. Bad telling deals with you just stating a fact about your character and then taking all the fun out of reading for your audience. Good telling involves using story context and, more importantly, interiority, to paint a three-dimensional picture where you make your reader feel the story experience, but you don't exclude them from participating, either." —*Mary Kole, literary agent and blogger at kidlit.com*

THIS CHAPTER PROVIDES fun and inspiring ways to describe a character's hair color. Not only can a character's facial features tell the reader a thing or two about them, but their hair color can also reveal things about the characters in any fictional world.

One way to describe a character's hair color is to be creative and not use boring descriptive words. Natural hair color is usually black, blonde, brown, gray, or red.

BELOW THE FIRST examples all state a fact and describe the character in a bland way. I'll do my best to revise each one to enhance the descriptions.

Please review these examples...

BLAND: Mary had short, blonde hair.

REVISED: Mary's shorn, brassy locks cupped her oval face.

BLAND: She had copper tones in her long hair.

REVISED: The sunlight highlighted the glossy copper tones of her long hair.

BLAND: She had wispy, dark colored hair.

REVISED: A strand of dark, wispy hair tumbled across her forehead.

BLAND: The slender girl had red curls.

REVISED: Soft red ringlets bounced off her slim shoulders.

I REALIZE that some of my revised writing examples aren't terribly creative, but they should still clearly show you how to fix any sentences with filter words or revise any bland descriptions into what could be considered a deeper POV.

I have included a list of colors in this chapter to provide creative and original ideas for describing a character's hair color.

Thesaurus of hair colors:

Highlights (blond, gold, black, red, auburn, etc.)

Arctic blond

Ash Brown

Ash-Blond

Auburn

Beige White

Black

Blonde

Brunette

Burgundy

Buttermilk

Butterscotch

Caramel

Chardonnay

Chestnut

Chocolate

Cinnamon

Copper

Coppery Red

Dark

Dirty blonde

Domino

Ebony

Fair

Fiery

Flame Red

Flaxen

Ginger

Golden

Gray

Honey

Honey Blonde

Irish Red

Jet black

Onyx

Golden Blonde

Pecan

Raven

Red

Russet

Salt and Pepper

Wine-Red

Wheat

Highlights

Sable

Tawny

PLEASE READ this short excerpt from my adult urban fantasy novel that describes a character and their hair.

Please review this descriptive writing example...

Her midnight hair draped around her shoulders like a glossy veil and her lab coat clung to her curvaceous figure. Necole's brown eyes swirled with green flecks and her brown skin glistened under the fluorescent lights. I wondered how she could stand so long in those last season Prada heels.

THE INFORMATION in this chapter should inspire you to be original and creative when you're describing a character's appearance.

32

Describing Apparel

"YOU CAN QUICKLY CONVEY a number of things about your characters based on the clothing they wear. For example, think about a wealthy person and how that person might dress. You may have imagined a man in an expensive suit or a woman in designer clothes. You can immediately signal to your reader that a character is wealthy with markers such as these." —*author, Bridget McNulty*

AH, fashion...one of my favorite subjects! I've always loved clothing, shoes, and accessories.

Now that I write full-time, I mainly live in sweatpants and pajamas. Everything I knew about being a full-time writer, (*thank you very much, Carrie Bradshaw*), was from watching movies and TV shows. And the longer I work at home, the lazier I get about my appearance. Whatever clothes I wake up in are only seen by my family, or by the occasional neighbor who catches a glimpse of me through the windows. Maybe you have a character like me, who works from home and lives in their pajamas.

This chapter examines clothing descriptions, and mainly focuses on modern garments for both male and female characters.

Describing a character's wardrobe might seem tedious or unneeded, but consider this, clothing reveals a great deal about a character, just as it does actual people. Even if you're not writing a fashionista, it's still good to know your character's personal style, which says a lot about who they are, their social status, age, and profession. Plus, our clothing choices are often an expression of our distinct individuality, so like real people, characters should dress to match their unique personalities.

Clothing descriptions can be a powerful and effective visual for the reader. This is especially helpful if you write in the young adult genre. Most teens like to express themselves though fashion.

Here is a reference list that should help with fashion descriptions. In case you aren't current on fashion verbiage, this terminology should be used as a general indication for many different time periods and genres.

THESAURUS OF CLOTHING styles and types:

Preppy: Plaid Skirts, Sweater Vests, Pearl Necklaces, Big White Sunglasses, Sportswear, Casual Lifestyle Apparel, Outdoor Gear, Classic, Bold Colors, Prints

Punk: Streetwear, Skinny Jeans, Leather, Studded belts, Ragged T-shirts or Jeans, Casual, Bright Colors, Prints, Jackets, Chinos

Modest: Long Skirts, Sweaters, Long-sleeved Shirts, Feminine, Turtlenecks, Muted Colors

Sophisticated: Suits, Trousers, Pencil Skirts, Silk Blouses, Classic, Timeless, High-Fashion, Elegant

Sporty: Sweats, T-Shirts, Tennis Shoes, Sneakers, and Board-Shorts, Sportswear, Casual Apparel

Edgy/Emo: Skinny pants, Black Boots, Damaged Jeans, Tight T-Shirts, Studded Belts, Doc Martens Boots, High-Top sneakers, Hoodies

Vintage: Retro, Florals, Cardigans, Classic, Bright Colors, Wild Prints, Second-Hand Clothing, Stylish, High-Street Fashion

Western / Wild West: Leather, Cowboy Boots, Bolo-Ties, Button-up Shirts, Wrangler Jeans, Hat

Nautical/Preppy: Blue, Red, and White colors, Bows, Flipped-up Collars, Polo Shirts

Summer Attire: Sandals, Sundress, Sandals, Flats, Floppy Hats, Shorts, Cut-offs, Flip-Flops

Futuristic: Metallic, High-Neck Collars, Mesh, Cyberpunk, Pullovers

Rocker: Band Logos, Skinny Jeans, Leather-Studded Belts, Scarfs, Leather Cuff Wristbands

Boho-Chic: Layered Clothing, Baggy Shirts, Big Purses, Long Necklaces, Ankle-Length Skirts, Bohemian, Hippie, Hand-crafted Clothes

Sexy: Low-Cut Dress, Mini-Skirt, Stilettos, Fishnet Stockings, V-neck Shirt, Trendy, Seductive, Sensual

Casual: Shorts, Pants, Tennis Shoes, Flip-Flops, Sweatpants, Hoodies, PJs

Formal: Floor-Length Gowns, Tuxedo, High-Heels, Wingtip Shoes

Casual Chic: Designer Jeans, Khaki Pants, Capris, Clingy Dresses

Hippie: Baggy Clothes, Peace Signs, Long Skirts, Bell-Bottoms, Tie-Dye

Dressy: Button-Down Shirts, Strappy Heels, Big Bags, Vests, Shirt Dress, Straight Legged Pants

Hip-Hop: High-Tops, Baggy Jeans, Oversized Shirts, Gold necklaces

Beach/Boho: Big Shades, Headbands, Sundresses, Khaki Shorts, Tank-Tops

HERE IS an excerpt from my adult cozy mystery novel that should be inspiring when describing your own characters and their fashion style.

Please review this descriptive writing example...

A smiling man in his early twenties stepped closer to me. "Greetings, I'm Bellamy. My deepest sympathies to you and your family." He had soft black curls and expressive, ocher eyes framed by thick lashes. His skin was a smooth brown and his style boho chic: a smoking jacket in gorgeous jewel tones over a tank top and dark chinos, with a colorful scarf draped around his neck, adding a flair of flamboyance.

BELOW I HAVE INCLUDED a wordlist of clothing and fashion styles that should be useful when describing a character's clothing.

Wordlist of clothing and fashion terms:

Baggy

Cheap

Mismatched Colors

Socks with Sandals

Ratty

Stained

Expensive

Chic

Tight-Fitting

Lagenlook Clothing

Gothic

Steampunk

Loungewear

Activewear

Adjustable

Adorable

Affordable

Asymmetrical

Banded

Beaded

Big & Tall

Blouse

Fur (faux or real)

Bold

Bootcut

Boxy

Breathable

Button-Down

Collared

Comfortable

Comfy

Contemporary

Cross-Stitched

Dapper

Delicate

Designer

Discounted

Distressed

Double-Breasted

Durable

Eco-Friendly

Edgy

Fitted

Flexible

Form-Fitting

Flowy

Hand-Sewn

Hand-Washed

Handmade

Jagged

Lined

Mini-Shirt

Minimalist

Modern

Organic

Professional

Push-Up Bra

Relaxed

Retro

Rugged

Semi-Formal

Short-Sleeve

Skinny-Fit

Skinny Jeans

Slip (undergarment)

Timeless

Tunic

Leather

Vintage

Water-Resistant / Waterproof

Casual

Minimalist

Formal

Plain

Western

Urban,

Tasteful

Maternity

Punk Rock

Military Fashion Style

Grunge

Flamboyant

Hip Hop Style

Street Wear

Kawaii Style

Unfashionable

Haute Couture

Artsy

Flashy

Glamourous

Cashmere

Boho Chic / Bohemian Style

Mohair

Classic

Classy

Embroidered

Everyday

Exotic

Fabric-Lined

Fancy

Fashionable

Faux

Feminine

Finely Detailed

Form-Fitted

Flattering

Flirty

Flouncy

Fully Lined

Funky

Gathered

Glamorous

Glitzy

Gypsy

High-Waisted

Imported

Ankle-Length

Innovative

Intricate

Knee-Length

Knit

Lacy

Layered

Lightweight

Loose

Flowing

Masculine

Metallic

Minimalist

Modern

Low-Cut

Skimpy

Old-Fashioned

Opaque

Open-Backed

Oversized

Patchwork

Patterned

Peasant

Petite

Pleated

Plunging

Practical

Pragmatic

Preppy

Pressed

Printed

Pull-On

Jumper

Pushup

Quilted

Racerback

Racy

Reinforced

Ribbed

Rocker-Style

Romantic

Scooped-Neck

See-Through

Sexy

Sheer

Silky

Soft

Simple

Sleek

Slimming

Slinky

Slip-On

Slouched / Slouchy

Snug

Sophisticated

Sporty

Stitched

Straight

Strapless

Strappy

Stretchy

Stylish

Supple

Symmetrical

Synthetic

Tailored

Textured

Tight

Trendy

Tunic Length

Unique

Vegan Leather

Versatile

Whimsical

Yarn-Dyed

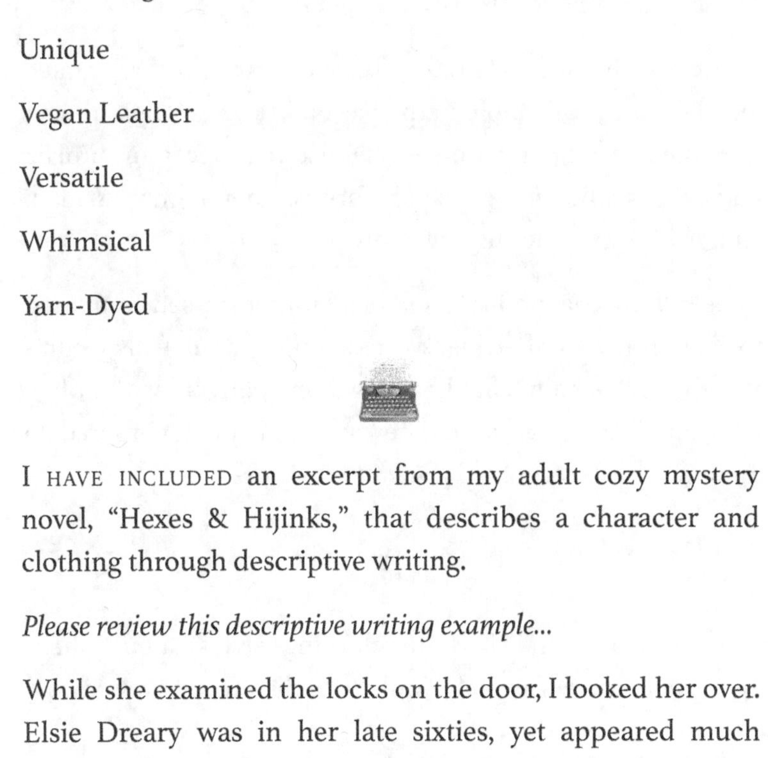

I HAVE INCLUDED an excerpt from my adult cozy mystery novel, "Hexes & Hijinks," that describes a character and clothing through descriptive writing.

Please review this descriptive writing example...

While she examined the locks on the door, I looked her over. Elsie Dreary was in her late sixties, yet appeared much younger. She had short, sunflower-blonde hair with soft bangs that swooped over cornflower-blue eyes and flaunted the striking symmetry of her face. I grinned at her purple fleece pajamas with a cupcake print under a plush robe and fluffy slippers. Wearing oddball PJs was one of her adorable quirks.

My own outfit wasn't quite as charming: an oversized sweater paired with black leggings and scuffed UGG boots.

I HAVE ADDED a brief excerpt from one of my sweet romantic comedy novels that describes characters and their clothing.

Please review this descriptive writing example...

As I open the door, I inhale a blast of warm, coffee scented air. He's sitting at a table in the back and waves when he sees me enter. Kyle's perfection—a handsome, successful broker, and impeccable metrosexual—dressed in a gray Armani suit. And my mother highly approves.

I peel off my coat and suddenly feel underdressed compared to Kyle in my somber black dress and cheap flats. My chin-length blonde hair is held back in a tiny ponytail with bobby pins and a rubber band. The only makeup I bothered to apply was waterproof mascara and lip-gloss.

THE EXAMPLES and lists on clothing styles should help portray characters as real people with distinct personalities.

33

Clothing & Fabrics

"Wʜᴀᴛ ᴅᴏᴇs ʏᴏᴜʀ ᴄʜᴀʀᴀᴄᴛᴇʀ *ʜᴇᴀʀ*? *Taste? Feel? See? Smell?* How does the breastplate feel on your character? What about chainmail? Is your steampunk character struggling with her corset? (I know mine does.) If you write horror and your character is buried alive, what sensory details will your character encounter that your reader might not be familiar with (and how can you use them to create terror)?" *—M. B. Weston, award-winning author of The Elysian Chronicles*

Tʜɪs ᴄʜᴀᴘᴛᴇʀ ɪs a great reference for describing characters, furnishings, and settings within your storyworld. Fabrics are used in clothing, furniture, décor, bedding, carpets, curtains, accessories, bandages, and even some forms of housing (tents).

There are many different ways to describe characters, and one way to do that is by describing a character's wardrobe.

Please compare these simple examples...

BLAND: Harry was a thin man who always wore a brown, tweed suit.

While it states a fact and describes the character, it's rather bland, isn't it? Let's see if I can improve this description.

REVISED: Harry's tweed suit was the color of burnt toast and his clothing sagged on his lanky frame.

Not great, but much better than the first example. Let's review more ways you can describe a character's fashion style and use fabrics in your descriptions.

HERE ARE two excerpts from my adult college romance novel that describe clothing, combined with the setting and the senses.

Please review this descriptive writing example...

The scent of *Eau de School*, a mixture of fried foods and mingled fragrances overwhelmed my senses. We shuffled forward with our trays, and I took in the room with its dull beige walls and crowded tables. A couple of students donned pajamas with various degrees of bedhead and five students in trendy clubbing attire seemed hung over, but the majority of people wore normal college garb: jeans, shorts, and wrinkled T-shirts.

Please review this descriptive writing example...

Brooklyn turned on her iPad. On her ears were diamond studs, flashing in the sunlight. She gave off this effortlessly street-chic vibe dressed in a stylish knit pullover with tight black jeans, leather knee-high boots, and a crocheted beanie that all screamed *money.*

BELOW I HAVE INCLUDED a wordlist of fabrics that should be useful when describing a character's clothing.

This list will also come in handy when describing objects, décor (furniture, drapes, bed linens, etc.), and settings.

Wordlist of fabrics and color styles:

Ornate

Acrylic

Alpaca

Angora

Applique

Rayon

Fuzzy

Argyle

Baize

Bamboo

Basket Weave

Batik fabrics

Blend (combination of two or more fibers within the same yarn)

Boucle

Broadcloth

Brocade (mainly used on furnishings)

Buckram (typically used in bookbinding and millenary)

Burlap

Calico

Cambric

Camel Hair

Canvas

Chambray

Chantilly Lace

Charmeuse

Chintz

Corduroy

Crochet

Damask (mainly used for draperies and home décor)

Delaine

Dobby

Double Knit

Felt

Flannel

Fleece

Gauze

Gingham

Gossamer

Herringbone

Ikat

Jersey knit

Kapok (mainly used as filling in mattresses, pillows, life vests, and upholstery.)

Lambswool

Lamé

Lycra

Metallic

Mesh

Microfibers

Net

Organza

Paisley

Sateen

Seersucker

Sequins

Taffeta

Tapestry

Tartan

Terry Cloth

Tie-Dye

Tulle

Upholstery

Velvet

Velveteen

Vinyl

Chenille

Egyptian cotton

Faille

Latex

Microfiber

Polyamide

Bark Cloth

Synthetic

Plaid (tartan cloth)

Polyester

Wool

Tweed

Color Block

Ponte Knit

Box Pleat

Chiffon

Denim

Crepe

Linen

Silk

Velour

Pashmina

Leather

Polka Dot

Suede

Floral

Checkerboard Pattern

Woolen Fabric

Felted Material

Satin

Cotton

Manufactured Fiber

Weave

Lace

Natural Hair Fiber

Woven

Knitted

Nylon

Spandex

Muslin

IF YOU ARE CRAFTING a scene using the five senses, "touch" is one that is frequently ignored. If you are describing a character's clothing, you could include a mention of the fabric and how it looks and feels to enhance the description or just depict the material.

This list can also be used to describe objects, weather, décor, animals, birds, reptiles, and settings.

Wordlist to use to describe a look, feel, or texture:

Accent

Coarse

Heavy

Thick

Eyelet

Rubber-Like

Embellish

Elastic

Decorative

Twill

Crispness

Silky

Sheen

Stretchy

Embossing

Absorbent

Crinkled

Rough

Shiny

Soft

Delicate

Hard

Cold (metal armor, breastplate, chainmail. Etc.)

Smooth

Bumpy

Abrasive

Supple

Strong

Stiffness / Stiff

Starched

Flamboyant

Durable

Flexibility

Dense

Embroidered

Wool-Like

Uneven Finish

Luxuriant

Wrinkled

Ironed

Comfy

Hairy

Plush

Itchy

Lightweight

Warm

Fluffy

Luxurious

Luster

Glossy

Elegant

Slippery (silk sheets)

Matte

Sleek

THIS EXCERPT IS from my urban fantasy novel, "Slayers & Spells," that laces "narrative voice" into the description of a setting, along with a character description, clothing, and a little humor.

Please review this descriptive writing example...

I parked outside the cemetery gates and hiked to the abandoned mortuary that the vampire squatters called home. I waited for Raze outside the building.

Crackling leaves and branches sliced through the hushed graveyard. My body jolted with instant jitters. I had the distinct feeling that it wasn't Raze. It could be a groundskeeper, or even the cops, all of which I was none too eager to see, or explain to the latter why I was loitering in the cemetery.

I ducked inside the funeral parlor, closing the door. Inside was dark and damp. Slices of sunlight streamed through a boarded window. I peeked through a slit.

Muted footsteps sounded from behind me and I whirled to face Karma, the same auburn-haired vampire I'd fought before.

Guess I should've waited outside.

Karma's outfit screamed: *I'm-a-classic-eighties-lover.* She wore an oversized blazer fashioned with shoulder-pads, ripped jeans, and Mondo Creepers. Her red hair was styled into a high-ponytail with a thick fringe of bangs.

"*You* again." Karma pushed up the sleeves of the blazer. "I'm a powerful immortal and you're only a weak girl—"

"Shut it, retro vamp." I summoned my natural magics "And I'm not weak. So, any last words before I stake you? Like I admit to being a clueless fashion victim?"

POWERFUL DESCRIPTIONS WILL GRAB a reader's attention and emerge them within your story by *showing* readers your extraordinary fictional world. Description is a crucial element of powerful storytelling.

Well, that's it for my advice on writing compelling descriptions. All of these tools and recommendations should really help you create dramatic scenes that will keep readers coming back for more.

Wishing each and every one you much success on your writing journey!

Humble Request

IF YOU READ this handbook and find the tools and tips helpful to improving your own storytelling abilities, please consider posting an honest review online.

Word of mouth is crucial for any author's success, and reviews help to spread the book love. Please consider leaving a short *(a sentence or two is fine!)* review wherever you purchased this copy and/or on Good-reads.

If I get enough reviews stating that this guide helped writers to hone their craft, then I'd love to include additional books in the Fiction Writing Tools series.

Author Services

I HAVE INCLUDED a list of services that I offer authors to help them along their creative journey. If you have any questions, please don't hesitate to contact me.

Pease visit my blog, "Fiction Writing Tools," for tons of advice on book promotion, author branding, and self-editing.

Developmental Editing: https://tinyurl.com/2s3krtfj

Discreet Ghostwriting Services: https://bit.ly/3QESgBI

The Plot Coven (Custom Plots): https://bit.ly/3U8uWOa

The Plot Coven Facebook group (Premade Plots & Concepts): https://bit.ly/3U7G121

Book Marketing Services: https://bit.ly/3G8Q5A5

Promotional graphics (*TikTok, Instagram, Facebook, or Twitter.*): https://bit.ly/3wmYHRJ

The Cover Coven (premade & custom book covers): https://tinyurl.com/2xmmj7t2

The Cover Coven Facebook group (monthly cover sales): https://www.facebook.com/groups/thecovercoven

Fun & Inspiring Creative Writer Notebooks: https://bookcover-designs.blogspot.com/p/writer-notebooks.html

Wishing you lots of prosperity, creativity, and positivity!

36

Fiction Writing Tools

Bestselling author S. A. Soule shares her expertise with writers by providing surefire, simple methods of getting readers so emotionally invested in their stories that booklovers will be flipping the pages to find out what happens next.

Each of these helpful and inexpensive self-editing books in the *Fiction Writing Tools* series encompass many different topics: dialogue, exposition, internal-monologue, setting, and other editing techniques that will help you take your writing skills to the next level.

THE WRITER'S GUIDE TO CHARACTER EMOTION

Updated 2022 Second Edition!

Most writers struggle with creating a captivating story. The fastest way to improve your writing is by the use of the "deep Point-of-View" technique, which can transform any story from mediocre storytelling into riveting prose.

This manual will provide writers with the essential skills needed to significantly enhance their characterization and intensify emotions by eliminating filtering words that cause narrative distance. Plus, this unique guidebook includes hundreds of amazing ways to use "show don't tell" to submerge readers so deeply into any scene that they will experience the story along with the characters.

THE WRITER'S GUIDE TO CHARACTER EXPRESSION

Updated 2022 Second Edition!

This book is a companion guide to the first volume in the Fiction Writing Tools series on descriptive writing and expands on this vast topic. You don't need to read the books in order, but I do suggest using both as references in your writer's toolbox.

This in-depth guide offers fiction writers practical tools on how to use descriptive writing to create realistic settings, visceral responses, and lifelike characters.

No matter what genre you write, this second handbook on writing powerful descriptions should be kept as a vital reference in every writer's toolbox. This helpful resource of endless inspiration will instantly help writers to hone their craft.

THE WRITER'S EASY & FUN SCENE REVISION WORKBOOK

This Scene Revision Workbook and Manual Can Take Your Writing Skills to the Next Level and Make the Editing Process Fun!

Every writer knows that scenes are the building blocks of every great story. Revision should be fun and never overwhelming.

Many of us have written a scene and felt as though it was lacking something. Or perhaps you wrote an entire novel, but want to know how to make it shine. This scene revision workbook can improve anyone's writing and works for every genre to ensure that every scene is stronger, purposeful, and impactful.

Using this scene revision workbook on my own publications has helped many of my fiction novels make it to the top 100 Amazon bestseller lists. It has also gotten me mostly 4 and 5 star reviews on my novels. It has honed my craft, so that I write books that readers really enjoy, and I know it will inspire you, too.

Whether you're writing your very first novel or your tenth, the self-editing advice provided in this revision guide and workbook can help writers keep their storyline on track, work through the revision process, and create page-turning prose. Also, includes ways to assess a draft for filler scenes, weaknesses, and common scene issues.

THE WRITER'S GUIDE TO BOOK COVER SECRETS

Frustrated with low book sales? Do you aspire to widen your audience and expand your readership? Have you tried and failed to get a Bookbub deal?

If you answered yes to any of those questions, then this book can help.

Most writers struggle with book promotion and attracting their target readership. In this remarkable and inexpensive guide, indie authors will learn amazing insider tips on book cover design, along with influential marketing tactics that will increase sales and catch the attention of readers.

A writer works hard on the "inside" of a book, so they should ensure that the "outside" is just as awesome.

The problem is that most self-published writers are unsure what "author branding" means. or how impactful a "genre specific" book cover is to the effective promotion of a book.

The best way to increase book sales, and save time and money on advertising is by using the secrets revealed in this handbook. The topics in this in-depth guide include powerful ways that authors of popular genres can attract more readers. If done right, a genre specific cover will sell itself and make a massive impact on a book's success.

THE COZY MYSTERY RESOURCE GUIDE

An invaluable resource on all things cozy mystery for writers of the genre!

This amazing handbook will save mystery and cozy mystery writers time and energy searching for resources to hone their craft and market their books.

In the reference section are links to online resources such as mystery plot outlines, reliable and professional services (designers, marketing, premade plots, editors, etc.), cozy and mystery groups on Facebook, online courses, inspirational videos, and recommended writing and plotting handbooks, along with a directory of promotional sites, and book reviewers and bloggers.

This guide also contains a list of tropes, themes, story prompts, crimes, settings, jobs, hobbies, keywords, subgenres, and so much more.

Plus, as a special bonus, this handbook includes interviews with some of the most respected and bestselling authors of the cozy genre today, offering inspiring advice and writing tips.

THE WRITER'S GUIDE TO REALISTIC DIALOGUE

A Powerful Reference Tool to Crafting Realistic Conversations in Fiction!

This manual is specifically for fiction writers who want to learn to create riveting and compelling dialogue that propels the storyline and reveals character personality.

Writers will also learn to weave emotion, description, and action into their dialogue heavy scenes. With a special section on how to instantly improve characterization through gripping conversations. All of these helpful writing tools will make your dialogue sparkle!

THE WRITER'S GUIDE TO CHARACTERS, PLOTS, & SCENES

A Simple System to Writing a Gripping Fiction Novel!

This plotting guidebook offers simple advice on creating stronger beginnings and lifelike characters. Writers will also learn to make their first pages so intriguing with chapter "hooks" that the reader won't be able to put the book down.

With easy to follow instructions on creating a comprehensive plot with the three-act structure and crafting realistic characters, writers of any genre will gain the tools needed to blend character goals and conflict to instantly strengthen the narrative.

Topics in this book include: 3 Extensive Creation Character, Templates, Tools to Create a Page-Turning First Chapter, Advice on Writing Scene Hooks, Simple Breakdown on Story Structure, Advice from Bestselling Authors on Plotting.

Whether you're writing an intense thriller or a sweeping romance, all novels follow the same basic outline described in detail within this book.

THESE GUIDEBOOKS ARE NOW ON SALE AT ALL MAJOR RETAILERS!

About the Author

S. A. Soule is a Creativity Coach, developmental editor, ghostwriter, and book cover designer, who has years of experience working with successful novelists. Many of her fiction and non-fiction books have spent time on the bestseller lists.

Her guidebooks in the "Fiction Writing Tools" series are a great resource for writers at any stage in their career, and they each offer helpful advice on how to instantly take your writing skills to the next level and successfully promote your books.

Please feel free to browse her blog, which has some great tips on creative writing online at: Fiction Writing Tools and a list of author services. And don't forget to browse around The

Cover Coven which has a large selection of book cover designs in every genre.

www.ingramcontent.com/pod-product-compliance
Lightning Source LLC
Chambersburg PA
CBHW071733150726
47998CB00005B/1619